GIRL FORWARD

ONE WOMAN'S UNLIKELY ADVENTURE IN MONGOLIA

HEATHER WALLACE

To Carol —
Enjoy the
journey!

Heather Wallace

Reviews for *Confessions of a Timid Rider*

"Heather Wallace reflects in this memoir how full life can be when one steps outside of her comfort zone to blaze her own trail. She writes with courage and self-acceptance while shining a light on how fear can get in the way of following a passion, (and how to overcome those fears). This uplifting book will touch anyone who loves writing, animals, and chasing after dreams," ~ Carly Kade, author of In the Reins, Cowboy Away, and Show Pen Promise

"Many women that I know have returned to their childhood passion for riding. They quickly learn that life is different at 40 than it was at 10! The author writes about her experience of returning to riding in a fun, light-hearted style that makes for easy reading. Several of you will be able to relate to her experiences."

~ M.J. Evans, author of In the Heart of a Mustang

"Sometimes in the equestrian world it seems like

everyone else has their act together except for me, [am I the only one whose car has arena grit on the floor and sports alfalfa bits in my purse)? Thanks to Heather's authenticity in storytelling, I feel less alone juggling the work/life/barn life situation. The chapter about her daughter as her hero is really special, and as tender as her voice can be, in other parts her fun, snarky side comes out, (but not too snarky). What I really enjoyed as I read this book is that I felt like she was having a conversation with me. Her voice is very strong, and she is not shy about delving into her personal joys and struggles. Timid rider or not, if you are a grown up horse girl who likes a good story, you'll feel like you made a new friend by reading Heather Wallace's memoir."

~ Susan Friedland-Smith, author of Horses Adored and Men Endured and blogger of Saddle Seeks Horse

"This is the perfect book for a summer afternoon. It's a quick and easy read with wonderful insights that easily translate into experiences everyone can relate to — not just riders. When I read Heather's story, it was surprising to me how similar her character is to my own and how often I recognized myself in her pages. I loved the way she tied the theme of each chapter to a life lesson. While of course she does refer everything

back to her experiences on horseback, her subtitled 'confessions' under each chapter heading in Part Two are easily extrapolated into everyday living. If there is one criticism, it is that I would have enjoyed seeing more photos of the animals and people she talks about! The final paragraph says it all and sums it up quite nicely, "Face your fears and push through them however you can to follow your passion!"

~ Sabine Schleese

"Heather P. Wallace's nonfiction memoir, Confessions of a Timid Rider, is a marvelous and inspirational work written by an author who has repeatedly faced her fears and accepted the inevitable setbacks as they occur and still has managed to live her dreams. I loved reading about her experiences with her horses, especially Earthly Delights. Her frank and honest discussions about anxiety and the "what-ifs" that can work to deprive one of their self-confidence are quite helpful, and I'm sure anyone who reads this remarkable book will see themselves in at least some of Wallace's work. Readers are fortunate indeed in Wallace's other love being writing, which she does well. Her memoir is a joy to read. I finished it having learned a lot about horse and equine behavior, but I also was a witness to her triumph over that timid aspect of herself on almost *every page. Wallace's courage and resilience is something to cheer about, and her memoir records it brilliantly. Confessions of a Timid Rider is most highly recommended."*

~ *Jack Magnus, Reader's Favorite.*

Reviews for *Equestrian Handbook of Excuses*

"A great, concise handbook of every excuse you can think of to NOT ride — from it being too cold to thinking that your four-legged friend is a bit too sleepy when you arrive at the yard... The Equestrian Handbook of Excuses has them all!!!"

~ *Sophie Tunnah*

"This handbook is adorable! I think I've used most of these excuses and found a few that I'll keep in mind the next time my barn mates try and get me on a trail ride when I'm just not feeling it. Wink wink. It would make a cute, inexpensive gift for someone who is discouraged in their riding or for someone who just needs a pick-me-up."

~ *MK Morris*

"Charming, witty, and exactly what we need on those

days we just don't feel it. Heather Wallace sums up all of these sentiments and simultaneously provides solidarity, humor, and encouragement to all the riders who feel this way from time to time."

~ *Lindsey Rains*

GIRL FORWARD

A Tale of One Woman's Unlikely Adventure in
Mongolia

by Heather Wallace

Publisher:

Heather Wallace/Water Horse Press LLC

Email: heather@timidrider.com

Ordering Information: Quantity sales are available for US trade bookstores and wholesalers. For details, contact the publisher at the address above. Printed in the United States of America.

ISBN 9781719204507

First Edition

Cover photos courtesy ©Heather Wallace/ Gobi Desert Cup

DEDICATION

To my husband and daughters. Thank you for understanding why I traveled across the world, for cheering me on, and for holding down the fort in my absence. Without you and your support, I wouldn't be able to follow my dreams.

FOREWORD

I have a story to share, a story about people who inspire us. The strong, inspirational, and fun mothers and entrepreneurs.

My name is Camille Champagne, and I am the Founder and Ride Director for The Gobi Desert Cup, a 480-kilometer endurance race in the vast Gobi Desert of Mongolia.

The Gobi Desert Cup is a race that invites riders and adventurers from the four corners of the world. It was founded in 2017 by Naranbataar Adiya and myself. We arc both passionate about Mongolia, the native horses, and horse racing. Nara is a veterinarian based in Mongolia. Myself, I am an international endurance rider based in Queensland, Australia.

It was indeed a very ambitious and great challenge to set for ourselves. In July 2018, my husband and I welcomed our first child. Charlotte arrived three weeks before the second edition of our annual event.

But I would like to talk about the people who support me, inspire me, and guide me through the successes of The Gobi Desert Cup and my journey as a new mother.

Only recently I have learned what it is to be a working mum: to work around your children, juggle the house chores, commitments, work, phone calls, meetings, answering emails, doctor appointments, and still find time to get some sleep.

In April 2018, I had the pleasure of meeting Heather Wallace from New Jersey. We were two women from two different cultures and countries. I was looking for a Media Coordinator and after seeing our ad, Heather emailed us. We considered her amongst a few other people. We interviewed Heather who was very interested as we were, knowing this was the start of a great journey.

Heather jumped on board not having prior experience in endurance riding nor traveling to Mongolia. You could say that she went right out of her comfort zone as she described herself and her blog, *The Timid Rider*.

Going away to a third-world country with only basic

amenities, lost in the Gobi Desert in the middle of an international race, for ten days was a challenge taken on by Heather.

I simply don't know how she managed to put in her heart, passion, and a whole lot of hard and consistent work for all these months. It was so easy for me to forget her other commitments. When we officially met in Asia after months of working together over the internet, it was real and weird; she was shorter than I imagined but greater than I could have hoped for.

Nothing was ever an issue, and everything had a solution; she was a great team player, and a huge happy everyday enthusiast. She quickly picked everything up and became confident in an environment where she wasn't familiar. From our veterinarians, chief steward, volunteers, riders, and all our Mongolian people, there was no doubt; we had just found the piece missing to make the Gobi Desert Cup a great success.

I gave birth to my baby not long before heading to Mongolia. Support from another mother during that time was priceless. It can be hard, and the guilt can make us doubtful about our work. It is refreshing to work with someone who lives life 100% and makes it look easy; it helps reshape your thinking. It certainly helped get me through a great challenge: leaving Australia, my husband, and our newborn baby to run the race on another continent. We all need someone to look up to, someone who has our back, someone who understands what it is to be a parent and a wife. Someone who understands that challenging doesn't mean impossible; it means more organization and taking more time to achieve it.

It was very stressful with a huge workloads, challenges, and little time to accomplish it all. Heather jumped onboard and had to very quickly adapt and start her duties.

If you wonder what a super hero looks like in daylight, well she is it. Married with three beautiful girls, two dogs, a horse, Heather also has a publishing business, is a qualified equine and canine sports massage therapist, a blogger, and award-winning author.

Heather, aka "Jersey" has taken our race to a whole different level with modern branding and marketing, including capturing the event in photography and sharing ride updates on social media. We now have great content and engagement from our followers. You can have an amazing passion for your business, but you need someone to translate it to the public and the media. Someone who can see your vision and what you are trying to achieve.

In our case, our mission is to provide sustainability to the nomadic people of Mongolia through the Gobi Desert Cup, which directly benefits the Mongolian

Horse and Nomad Foundation. We create more than 50 jobs for up to three months each year in Mongolia and hire 130+ horses. Once selected, the horses come to our training center and are supervised by our local veterinarian, Naranbataar Adiya. 90% of the people we employ are nomadic people, and the translators and the catering mob are from the capital, Ulaanbataar. The race has a huge economic and social impact on the local people. On top of that, it is an international endurance race that promises the adventure of a lifetime to riders from the four corners of the world! We share the journey of our riders from the minute they sign up and continue to offer support and advice.

For our new team member, it was a huge and somewhat crazy commitment as she was secluded from the modern world for ten days with very limited electricity and people she hadn't met before. Heather had to have an understanding for the project and work with people from the four corners of the world, and all of that within four months. Leaving her family for two weeks, her business, animals, and clients required some serious consideration and organization.

Sometimes in life things are just meant to be!

Heather very quickly became a great asset and facilitated our entire communication system, updating everything for the riders. The website looks amazing, and our Facebook page is informative, fun, and interesting with a great community and engagement! While in Mongolia it was very clear within a few days that Heather belonged in our team.

She was floating around camp every single day looking rather bubbly and glamorous (being glamorous, by the way, is a rare thing when camping with only the basics for almost two weeks straight. It slowly wears off as days goes by, for most of us anyway – but not Heather).

All the riders became fond of her and felt comfortable sharing their stories, even the shy ones. It became very personal, like a big family. You know when things are meant to be, and it all works perfectly? That's how it felt to all of us. It was the start of a great collaboration and friendship.

Being a mother and an entrepreneur is a daily challenge. We need more people like Heather in our community to empower women. Heather inspires us to follow our dreams and encourage other people around us. She has a way of spreading kindness and bringing the best out of everyone. Speaking her truth has a way of picking up people as they hit a wall. Heather has an innate ability to think outside the box and bend the rules, which allowed her to make Mongolia feel like home. We need to celebrate the people around us and encourage each other to do wonderful things!

- Had Heather been a media consultant for an international event before? NO
- Did she know anything about endurance racing? NO
- Had she been camping? NO
- Had she been to a third world country before? NO

But she took a chance, worked hard, did a lot of research, and it clearly paid off.

We all need to continue to reach for the stars throughout our lives, and Heather was a great reminder of that. We need to keep moving forward.

Whether you are an equestrian superstar or amateur, head to *The Timid Rider* blog, and help us to inspire other riders to do great things and follow their dreams, no matter how big or small.

If you are an entrepreneur, get in touch and share your journey. The journey of a thousand steps starts with one.

~ Camille Champagne

Ride Director, The Gobi Desert Cup

FEI 3* Endurance Rider

AN UNLIKELY ADVENTURER

Sitting on the unique mix of grass, rock, and sand, I look out in the distance. I've traveled the world but nothing before could compare to the view before me. As I sift my fingers through the ground, it strikes me that it likely holds secrets of nomads and travelers before me. Did they feel the same thing? Were they struck by how small they felt, looking 50 kilometers or so into the horizon as the sun began its lazy descent? Did they feel alone? Or, like me, did they instead connect with themselves and imagine the possibilities?

Perhaps some travelers would be bored, staring at seemingly nothing as they rode the sturdy Mongolian horses for an entire day without spotting another human being.

I look to the south while sitting outside the door of my ger, a large round tent commonly used as a residence by the nomads, at basecamp. The doors always face south or southeast. There, the herders check the traditional horse line and begin to loosen the horses from the line for the evening, giving them freedom to wander and graze in the night. Some wear hobbles and others are haltered two-by-two to prevent them from going too far from camp. If there is water nearby the horses are content to stay close, and I look forward to hearing them outside the ger while I sleep. I make a note to wear my headlamp if I need the bathroom so I don't accidentally run into one and scare the both of us.

This moment of quiet contemplation gives me a much-needed reprieve and chance to acknowledge how lucky I am to be an unlikely adventurer here in the innermost regions of Mongolia. My family and friends were shocked when I announced that I would be traveling to Asia, camping, and working with an endurance horse race. After all, those things are completely outside my comfort zone. Yet here I am and loving every moment.

With a deep breath of the dry air, I stand, sore from carrying my heavy camera all day and helping at the veterinary checkpoints. Wiping off the dust, I look to the marquis where all the riders who have been drawn to this adventure have gathered for the evening debriefing, meal, and perhaps some entertainment in the form of stories, cards, and drinking. We make our own entertainment without electricity. Somehow, despite coming from seven different countries, we have formed a community for these ten days in the desert. Men and women, speaking different languages, ranging in age from 24 to 72-years old, but all united in our love of and thirst for adventure.

The Gobi Desert Cup has a tendency to do that. While I am new this year, and on a trial basis as the writer and photographer, I can see how close-knit the core group of officials and herders are. Despite language barriers, and despite incredible distance 11 and a half months of the year, this event draws people together. I am lucky to be part of it, even if it challenges me in every possible way.

Once upon a time there was a woman who questioned whether she was good enough but chose to try anyway. This is the story of an unlikely adventurer. This is my story.

IN THE BEGINNING

I n the beginning, I was a headstrong young girl with an independent but introverted streak. My name is Heather Wallace. My whole life I've loved books and horses, but I've never been 100% confident that I was talented in either aspect. Most people who meet me never know that this laughing, smiling face hides an incredibly shy woman who has felt criticized her entire life. Most introverts, which I am, hide because society rewards the extroverts. I learned to adapt in order to be heard in my home and became overly perky partly from nerves and because I was tired of people assuming I was a snob. My comfort zone involves reading a book on the couch in silence while my dogs rest, sprawled under my feet. Or alternatively, I love arriving at the barn hours before anyone else to enjoy the quiet nickers and sounds of grazing, flies buzzing around my head.

Social interactions must be prepared for, and often the aftereffect is complete and utter exhaustion, complemented by wondering why I would possibly say that awkward thing, and wondering if everyone thought I was insane. That is not to say, of course, that I do not love a good social setting! While I am quite happy on my own in a hermit cave of my own making, sometimes I crave noise, energy, and friends. It's just that these instances take a little work for someone who is inherently introverted.

If you can relate, know that I appreciate you. If you don't, perhaps you may better understand that quiet person, standing on the edges of the group, just observing.

But this story isn't about my beginnings; it is about my present, even if it is all connected.

———

THERE WAS NOTHING I WANTED MORE IN LIFE THAN TO have a family. I realize that no family is perfect, and of course mine is not either. But I understood from an early age how important family is to me, and this includes the family of my heart, not necessarily blood. I may have trouble showing affection because of my introverted nature, but I feel deeply and my loyalty is absolute.

When my husband and I met at a mutual friend's birthday event in New York City, I was suggestively dancing with his friend. I think I told my partner, "Just stand there, I'll dance." No one has ever accused me of not speaking my mind. I definitely made an impression. It didn't hurt that I was in a social mood, wearing a corset, and dancing like a maniac for fun. My future husband had his eye on another friend of mine until she left and I drew his notice, sassing him about his favorite hobby.

Poor man. You see, I never hold back. When I'm social I am all out. When I'm antisocial, I'm all in. I tend to be decisive, daring, and sometimes spontaneous but only when the mood strikes.

Luckily, that is the same person he fell in love with because I never plan to change. He learned early on that I was independent and bold. Good thing, because I've proven time and again that I am my own person who chooses to be married and chooses him over and again. My personality is such that I could never be with someone who doesn't understand that about me.

That isn't to say our marriage is perfect, because, let's face it, whose is? We have ups and downs, but there is a mutual respect and no desire to change the other. That is the same respect that keeps me married when he gets mad that I had an appointment for one small tattoo and came back with two tattoos, one of which is the opposite of small but says, "Love her or leave her wild."

This same basis for our relationship means that while we love spending time together, he encourages me to travel with friends and will also do the same. So, when I was approached about the idea of traveling to Mongolia with people I didn't know, for a horse race I had no experience with, he shrugged and said, "You've got to try."

He totally gets me.

It started off with a simple Facebook tag from an equestrian photographer I know through social media. There was an ad posted looking for a blogger to document this big event in Mongolia through writing and photography. Something about it made her think of me and she commented that she couldn't go, but would I be interested?

Surprisingly, I was interested. My travel time had lessened greatly with motherhood and with the exception of a few family vacations or weekends away, I'd only had one big international trip. And while Mongolia had never remotely been on my radar, I began to think seriously about it. I asked for more information which was sent via a form email on Mailchimp, and I did what any smart woman would do – I stalked the event and the organizer on the web to determine if this was legit. I was intrigued but didn't want to get pulled into something that celebrates risk to horse or rider, nor something that would put myself at risk in any way.

More, while I never ask permission, I did consult with my husband to see what he thought about my potentially being involved. It felt abstract and unlikely, but I wanted it with a fervor that surprised me. After all, I'd never had the inclination to travel to Asia nor heard about endurance racing.

In many ways I think my husband knew I would apply but didn't necessarily think I would get the position to work with The Gobi Desert Cup. The joke was on him, because within one week I'd submitted my application with links to my writing and photography portfolio and secured a two-hour Skype call with the co-founder. By the end of the call, she offered me the position and I was in.

———

AT THE SAME TIME THIS OPPORTUNITY AROSE, MY fledgling business partnership with a friend ended badly. She had given me the idea for the business so when I decided to pursue it, I asked if she wanted to do it together. We were excited and moon-eyed, but my husband warned me of the pitfalls of working with friends. I was idealistic and positive, so I took what he said and decided to try anyway.

I think that I knew when going through the certification program that I'd made a mistake. We stayed together, hotel rooms next to each other, and got along wonderfully. It never occurred to me to share a room, and she thought it may be good to have space from each other. As an introvert, I totally understood.

But a few days in, her frustration with the program grew. She began to mutter under her breath and loudly complain, which I found quite embarrassing. We were paying good money to be there, and I was happily learning everything I could. The other student equine massage therapists and I all got along wonderfully. I found myself wanting to apologize or explain her temper tantrum but chose not to. It wasn't my place, and frankly, I was baffled.

I loved her as a friend and I even appreciated the frustration with herself and the program. That being said, her reaction made me wonder if I was making a mistake. I felt it was too late to turn back and chose to overlook it as growing pains. After all, nothing is perfect.

For the next 18 months we struggled to work together. We had regular meetings and wrote to-do lists. Slowly we did grow clientele, mostly people that I knew from my barn or were friends with on Facebook. Retrospectively, all our clients were people that I had somehow found and encouraged to book with us.

I felt increasingly like I was focused on the business, knowing my husband gave me a three-year deadline to make money or I would have to go back to a 9-5 job to contribute to the household income and take some of the pressure off him. While I, of course, want to support my family, I love working for myself. I am fulfilled by working with animals and being my own boss, plus I can make my own hours and be home for my children every afternoon.

My business partner and I struggled as friends for a while. Instead of spending time socially, we spent more time talking business. She had another part-time job and had changing hours, so it was hard to book her clients and I never felt like she really cared if the business was successful because she always had something else to fall back on. To me, it felt like it was a hobby for her that she could give up any time. While I know for a fact she did care, I was upset and feeling resentful for all the hard work I put in, and yet it was still all falling apart.

Our business grew slowly, and we found ourselves resenting each other. I was at the same time running a blog, which was gaining in notoriety, and working on a book, *Confessions of a Timid Rider*. The blog was initially suggested by a client who always had interesting questions, and I thought it would be a great way to promote our business. My partner wanted nothing to do with it and it grew in scope, and frankly, in workload. I was having a lot of fun.

Running a business is hard. Running a business and building a clientele on virtually no advertising budget, with a friend, is almost impossible. Looking back, we likely didn't stand a chance. Our personalities were so different, and working with friends is almost always a bad idea.

One day I got a telephone call from a long-standing client that we donated our time to. It was volunteer work at a local therapeutic riding facility but it gave us regular work helping these animals. The temperature had dropped, and my partner cancelled last minute without offering to reschedule.

Sadly, this wasn't the first time she had cancelled a client or not followed up with a paying client. It was starting to become obvious that working together was not working out and we had different levels of investment. Sure, if it is below, say 20 degrees Fahrenheit, the muscles are too tight and it is best to reschedule, but it wasn't near that and we work with animals in all weather.

I asked my partner to meet me for a drink, but she refused. I think she knew that I was going to suggest we dissolve the partnership. It was more and more clear that neither of us were happy.

Sadly, it seemed to take a personal turn. She refused to meet me, and we proceeded to dissolve the business over text and email, something which grieved me. How could two adults run a business like this? I was incredibly shocked and saddened. I know that I had made mistakes, but to not be able to meet and discuss things together cemented the end. I felt like a complete failure.

The feeling was akin to what I imagine going through a divorce is like, and I had no idea how to handle it. I tried my best to be professional. I took the personal out, sought a lawyer's guidance, and offered to buy the business.

That did not go well at all. Things escalated and she

decided that we had to completely dissolve the partnership rather than let me buy her out. I started the painful process and closed the business myself, shutting down the website, closing the bank account, and sending her a check for half by certified mail to guarantee that she received it.

It was a really dark time.

I couldn't eat, I could barely sleep, and I cried all the time wondering what I did wrong but knowing I tried my best for as long as I could.

I know that I made mistakes. It was my first business; I'd researched and taught myself everything. But it was just a business. My friendship wasn't just dead. It was lit on fire and sent out to sea.

It wasn't possible to close everything overnight. It took over a month to do it correctly, and during that time, I mourned the loss of my friend. I just wanted to be done with it and start over.

With this chaos and feeling of failure happening in my life, part of me realized that Mongolia and the work with this endurance event was a new opportunity to spread my wings and have something positive to focus on instead of dwelling as I was on the loss of my relationship and business. I've never been comfortable with pessimism and feeling sorry for myself. More, I like a good challenge! I knew that traveling to Asia to work with The Gobi Desert Cup would be an adventure and give me something positive to focus on.

I had faith that everything would work out.

3

SETTING GOALS

I have never been the type of person who wins at raffles or games of chance. At the risk of sounding new-age bohemian, the best things happen organically. In 2018, I set a number of goals for myself, which included spending more time on photography; improving my video skills; being on camera more for *The Timid Rider* blog; public speaking; working with more brands; releasing a new book; and buying a horse! I am an overachiever in many ways. Unfortunately, that is the basis of a lot of my anxiety about being a perfect rider. All my goals centered on one thing and one thing only, stepping out of my comfort zone and challenging myself.

Did I complete all my goals? I knocked them out of the park, but some in unexpected ways.

Horse Ownership

Shortly after I published my goals for the year on the blog, my husband gifted me with the pony of my dreams, Ferrous. I fought for that pony, but he was a gift all the same. I could not envision a more perfect partner than him. While I have a true and abiding love for Delight, the off-track thoroughbred I trained on for two years, it became clear that he was too much of a challenge for me after I fell and broke my ribs. I needed to go back to basics, and while it wasn't his fault that I fell, I found myself backing off of him when I needed to keep moving forward. It was a subconscious action that made me disappointed in myself.

Delight was a young horse, and while calm and predictable, he was green and still in training. That is why I was so proud of myself for even coming as far on him as I did. But he needed a firm hand, and I was not providing it as I should after my injury. So, I rode a few lesson horses in the following months before my trainer asked me to ride Ferrous.

The barn owner's favorite, Ferrous was only allowed to be ridden by few and with a close eye. He was a Hunter champion, a flashy red roan with a lot of personality. My trainer put me on him, and he was markedly different from what I was used to in Delight.

Delight is 16.3 hands and very long, so he was a lot of work to collect into a frame. Because he was naturally balanced, I could drop my reins and ride straight with minimal effort as long as he was moving – he had two gaits: pokey and gallop. In between took a huge amount of leg.

Ferrous, on the other hand, was head shy and kept moving away from the mounting block. When under saddle, he was very unbalanced and challenging to keep straight. My whole body had to be perfectly set up to keep him aligned. But we fit. At 14.2 he fit my small stature like Delight never did, and we just clicked. Sometimes everything falls into place.

I learned quickly how to hold Ferrous together, and when we tentatively jumped over a few cross rails, something I hadn't the nerve to do since my fall, I laughed at the feeling of trust I felt for him.

While anyone could ride Ferrous, it became clear that not everyone could ride him well. He is sensitive, and the barn owner wanted someone for him that would not undo his training or teach him bad habits. More than anything, I felt he would be the perfect fit for my family. My trainer agreed; he was the perfect amount of challenge.

It took less convincing than anticipated when I asked

my husband to come see this pony. Perhaps he'd been exhausted or perhaps he too felt the fit was right, but within days Ferrous was mine. Shoot, I mean ours. I keep forgetting I need to share with my daughters!

Quickly I went from riding once per week in a lesson to riding two to three times weekly. I learned to feel how Ferrous would be that day when I first mounted. Would he be looky and slightly spooky, or would he be pokey and hard to move forward? The first thing I addressed was him being head shy. From years of being in the lesson barn and having kids waving their hands in his face or pushing him away when he got mouthy, this pony would anticipate and raise his head at the first sign of a hand.

This schoolmaster had much to teach me about my equitation, and we learned together how to trust each other. This, more than anything, was a gift that I'd always sought with horse ownership, and it is the reason that I've progressed so much this year in my riding and confidence.

Conferences

My goal was to not only attend a pet blogging conference but also attend my first American Horse Publications conference. Freelance writing was something I wanted to work on more during the year. Being so new to the equestrian industry, I relished the idea of meeting and learning from veterans from all aspects of the media industry and the equestrian world. I was terrified.

Why?

I am quite shy in new situations and I knew only two people, both of whom I'd never met in real life. I am much more content in small groups, but in situations where a lot of people know each other and I need to introduce myself, it is quite scary. Anticipation has always been a source of anxiety for me.

I love conferences for both the education and the chance to network and meet interesting people. I never want to stop learning. The equestrian world is small, and if you doubt it, simply attend one of the AHP conferences where everyone knows everyone else. It's only slightly intimidating. But still, I found friends and met new ones. The only real hiccup was the first dinner when each person was asked to stand up in front of the room and introduce themselves. I would gladly talk about anything but myself. It makes me incredibly uncomfortable and feels oily, like I'm selling myself. So, for about half an hour I sweated and nervously went over in my head what I would say, only to stand up and hear my voice tremble as I did. Hopefully I was the only one to notice.

Public Speaking

Did I mention I'm uncomfortable talking about myself? Meeting new people and in front of the camera is one thing. Well, if that makes me nervous you can imagine the anxiety public speaking gives me. In college at the University of Delaware, I pretended to have a kidney infection to avoid giving an oral exam. Sorry, but I am not sorry. But the reality is that in life you will likely be required to speak in public.

While working in scientific, technical, and medical publishing, I often attended and led board meetings, as well as met with high profile clients like the American Cancer Society where I would give presentations. Fear of public speaking could never be an option. How could I ask leading cancer surgeons from around the globe to work with me on a medical journal if I could not earn their respect and lead them accordingly?

I began to move up the publishing ladder and increasingly give presentations. In an effort to improve myself and face my fears, I went to the zoo.

You heard me correctly, I went to the zoo.

How did the zoo help me become better at speaking in

public? I love animals. It's easier to speak on something about which you're passionate. Not that I wasn't passionate about production deadlines and peer review. These things mattered to me and my job, but they weren't my true passion.

As a docent at the Central Park Zoo, I learned to speak publicly through the penguin feedings. This was the perfect start. The penguin exhibit is dark and only a limited number of people can attend. More, the attendees were all facing the opposite direction. I was, in many ways, free to speak without eyes on me. While the talks were scripted, I became increasingly comfortable to inject a little joke or two, making it my own. But it did the trick. My paralyzing fear was gone, and this helped me overcome the hurdle. I soon graduated to the sea lion feedings which gathered hundreds upon hundreds of zoo goers and passing tourists. Each time I became less nervous and had more fun with it. Instead of feeling trepidation, this became something I would look forward to each day.

While I still get nervous before speaking to a crowd, it is now a normal anxiety that I will trip and fall or basically look like an idiot rather than a paralyzing fear. And if I were to trip, or stumble with my words, I've learned that I can be myself and make a joke out of it but then continue moving forward.

I wanted to do more speaking events to challenge myself. So, I made it happen! I applied to speak at the BlogPaws pet blogging conference on the topic of Blogging to Books. Many people are surprised to hear that I have only been blogging two years but have published two books within that time. My talk was how I did it and how I could help others to do the same, because writing a book is a goal for many writers. While I made mistakes, I also learned from them, but I know much from working in the publishing world for over a decade.

The session went well, and people were seated on the ground to come hear me, so I feel it was a success. I look forward to learning more and challenging myself with more talks and presentations.

Video

Video is not my strong suit. I joke often that I'm inept at video behind the scenes *and* in front of the camera! I believe this is a trait inherited by my father who is famous for videotaping the ground.

I have all the tools at my disposal and because of photography, a pretty good idea for detail. However, I never seem to get it right! I either have perfect stabilization but no sound, or perfect sound and alignment but press record at the wrong time (blooper). Yes, it's a fact that I often record the ground on accident, an important foreshadowing for the future. I knew coming into the Gobi Desert Cup that this would be a challenge for me, but one I was willing to take on.

On Camera

I think I'm horribly awkward on camera. I've got a goofy, slightly dorky personality which is then compounded by the fact that when I feel nervous, I ramble. Like most introverts, I feel more comfortable behind the camera.

Fun fact: My mother had this grandiose idea that her teenage daughter with braces, Sally Jesse Raphael glasses, and permed hair could somehow be a model at five feet tall. Bless her heart but suffice it to say that my "agent" stole her money and I really had limited work. I did a little commercial modeling, but mostly the highlight of my career was joining a public television kid's show called *Kiddeo Video* filmed in Hazlet, New Jersey. It was a play-off of *You Can't Do That on Television*, and while a lot of fun to do, hardly brag-worthy.

Once in high school, a boy came up to me and told me he'd seen me that weekend on the public station that he was watching while sick, and then he proceeded to tell everyone. I was mortified. Teenagers can be tough. Luckily, I had tough skin and laughed it off but was grateful during the 1990s that the internet wasn't available. If someone, somewhere finds a single episode of this it will be a miracle, and I'd love to see it. I never wanted to be an actress, but I had a lot of fun doing the filming and meeting these other kids. Ironically enough, two decades later I would move to the same town as one of my former cast members who played for the Middletown South Football team. I'm sure his teammates would have had a good time teasing him as well.

So why the discomfort in front of the camera? I find it hard to take myself seriously or believe that anyone would actually want to watch me. Still, no one can say that I don't push myself out of my comfort zone.

Working with Brands

Each year I limit the number of brands I work with through my blog, *The Timid Rider*. It began the first year as *Bridle & Bone*, and my knowledge base was limited as were my page views. I had little experience and felt inadequate to work with brands. I focused more of dog brands because I did not yet have a horse of my own. In addition, I'm highly selective as what brands best complement my audience.

In 2018 I rebranded my blog to *The Timid Rider* due to both personal and business reasons, and I began to focus on equestrian-related brands with the new addition to our family, Ferrous. I am still extremely careful with whom I work, both on the blog and in life.

Books

Halfway through 2018 I released my memoir, *Confessions of a Timid Rider*, which was a huge goal of mine. While the book uses my personal experiences with horses as a metaphor, it is the perfect book for anyone who has ever been afraid to fail but determined to succeed. Challenging myself and overcoming my own feelings of inadequacy are things I feel very passionate about. Sharing my story and my very personal feelings with the world, however, was opening myself up to a lot of criticism.

Despite multiple rounds of editing by myself and others, the early published version was riddled with typos and a few formatting errors as well. In my haste, I neglected to push the publication date and as a result did not realize the errors until after the first printed copies were published. It was horribly embarrassing and taught me a harsh lesson.

Writing this book was a goal of mine for many years. To complete it and to publish it were a lot of work and something for which I am incredibly proud. I certainly made mistakes, which I learned from, and hope to never repeat again. But as horrible as it felt to make such a public mistake, I turned it into a learning experience and hopefully others will grant some leeway if they received an early copy and my sincere apologies.

That book, *Confessions of a Timid Rider*, is the cornerstone for my blog as a returning adult equestrian and pulled from the blog itself. While I experienced anxiety as a child and stepped away from horses as a result, my passion drove me back. I still experience moments of anxiety and self-doubt in all areas of my life – horses, business, motherhood, and marriage – but I refuse to let it hold me back and keep me from trying.

In many ways, writing and publishing this honest memoir allowed me to open the doors to other experiences that I never would have considered nor imagined. After all, if I could successfully write and publish a book, a goal of mine for my entire life, what couldn't I do? To have it received as a "Hot New Release" on Amazon, become a bestseller in three categories, and win an award for the Equus Film Festival is affirmation that I need to keep going.

Never had I envisioned traveling to Mongolia as a goal,

nor did I know how it would change me. And yet, when the opportunity arose, I grabbed it. My work life was suddenly expanding organically, and all the hard work I'd done seemed to be paying off. I was determined to say yes to every opportunity.

And so, I took a chance.

4

TAKING CHANCES

I never considered myself a risk taker, nor would most people mistake me for one. My husband loves extreme sports and is an adventurer by nature. He loves being active and doing new things, but I am quite the opposite usually.

Our summers on the beach generally involve my laying on the sand and reading while he frolics in the ocean for hours on end or goes running along the water's edge. He is the yin to my yang. I prefer adventures in stories and in my imagination rather than physical exertion and promise of death.

Our honeymoon was a glaring example. I love to travel. My father is a retired Air Force Captain and we would often journey as children on cross country road trips or via plane. In junior high, I spent weeks exploring

Europe and experienced other cultures and ancient history with wide, fascinated eyes.

My husband's family was a little more homebound and with the exception of a spring break to Jamaica in college, he had never traveled out of the country. As a result, we opted to go big and travel to Australia after our wedding.

We had it all mapped out and our first stop was Brampton Island, part of the Whitsunday Islands on the southern end of the Great Barrier Reef. We arrived in Cairns, after almost 22 hours of non-stop travel across the world and the Pacific Ocean, tired but energized for our adventure! We checked in with the appropriate travel company for our boat trip to the island, when surprise!

Instead of a boat ride, we were upgraded to a complimentary helicopter ride.

Fantastic.

Did I mention that I am terrified of heights? Yes, my father was a pilot, and I love flying in big planes. But small planes, no thank you. And helicopters, never. My father was adamant that these were the most likely to crash and burn, and as a former pilot who also worked in the aviation insurance industry, I listened to his advice.

I tried to back out.

My husband was all for riding in a helicopter and has never said no to adventure.

But alas, we were upgraded, the boat had left, and it was the helicopter or nothing. I white-knuckled it across the ocean and honestly barely breathed.

This was the first of many anxiety-inducing but adventurous moments on this trip. There were swimming with sharks, scuba diving, hiking to the top of the island, encountering spiders of extraordinary size, and so much more. I love the idea of adventure, but the reality is terrifying, and I was a ball of nerves the entire time. I faced a lot of fears and lived to tell the tale, so I call it a win. I'd like to think I learned a lot about myself on my honeymoon. I certainly learned my limitations and that my husband not only pushes me to challenge myself but gives me opportunities to do so.

Over the years there have been big and small challenges that I faced, some not of my own choosing as life tends to bring surprises. Especially when you are a mother. Still, we do what we can to face them. Motherhood and marriage are their own types of adventures, but my traveling became limited.

Then something extraordinary happened. Another equestrian blogger on Facebook tagged me in a post.

An equestrian adventure company was looking for a blogger for their next event taking place in Mongolia. At this point it was April, but I was sufficiently intrigued. I mentioned it to my husband and asked his thoughts.

The true adventurer that he is, he encouraged me. Jason always has my back and knew that I would go anyway but that it would cause friction. Yes, I'm stubborn but not unfeeling. If he had true concerns, I would listen, but I will always make my own decisions.

And so I began to research a little more about the event. I knew the basics. The Gobi Desert Cup is an endurance multistage race over 480 kilometers and six days on Mongolian horses throughout the Gobi Desert. Co-founded by Camille Champagne and Mongolian veterinarian, Naranbaatar Adiya, the inaugural race was in 2017, so this would only be its second year.

Riders from all over the world are chosen from applicants to compete individually and in teams of four. The living quarters are basic, tents without electricity or running water. The riders and officials very much live a nomadic lifestyle while on this journey.

The role they were looking for was someone to document the second race with writing and photography, something that I could certainly provide!

The only thing I knew was in my comfort zone was the word horse. Everything else was new to me: Mongolia, endurance, competition, and camping. Still, I felt compelled to apply. Before I submitted my application, I checked again with my husband and asked him if he'd be okay without me for two weeks in August. Because if I was going to try for this job, I wanted to be able to commit on the off-chance that I was chosen.

With my husband's support, I submitted my application and after about a week I was invited to interview via Skype with the co-founder Camille Champagne.

Camille has traveled the world and she is fearless in many ways. As an FEI 3* endurance rider competing globally, she rides horses that I've only dreamt of and for incredibly long distances. In her early 20's Camille left her native France and moved to Australia's Outback with only $100 dollars and the promise of a job. She built the life she wanted. But she took a huge chance to do it. It's never easy to leave your comfort zone, much less make a success of it.

Her motto is, "Mongolian will test you."

With my notebook ready to jot down notes and my stomach in my throat, we spoke for hours! While she is quite private, she shared some important details of her life with me in her fun French-Australian accent. I immediately was struck by Camille's passion for her sport and her event, and it made me want to be part of something so special. I had a lot of ideas and although I knew it would be an incredible amount of work, I wanted to be part of The Gobi Desert Cup and Camille's vision.

But I had to break my news to my husband. It is one thing to say, "Of course you should try darling." Now suddenly, it was real. I would be traveling 9,000 miles to the innermost regions of remote Mongolia, a vast and underdeveloped country nestled snugly between Russia and China. I would be camping, something which I do not do nor ever desired. In fact, my husband begged me for years and I would scoff. I knew I could care for myself with people I've never met while in these remote places. No, the most terrifying thought my husband probably had was realizing that he would have complete care of our three beautiful daughters for two whole weeks.

Oh, boy.

As much as I took a chance applying for such an adventure outside my comfort zone, in many ways Camille took a chance on me. All she knew about me was my application and social media. We never met in person; we didn't know people in common. But after our interview, Camille offered me the opportunity to join as the blogger and Media Consultant and I jumped at the chance. I just knew that this was something I had to do.

For me, I felt only excitement. I had four months to prepare and I began immediately. I researched Mongolia and the race. I spoke regularly to Camille and began work immediately to source riders and revamp the social media.

I had a goal, and one that fired me up.

I was taking a chance on The Gobi Desert Cup, and The Gobi Desert Cup was taking a chance on me.

5

PACKING

In case you have not yet realized it yet, I can be Type A when it comes to certain things. I find that keeping organized and planning helps to keep my anxiety in check. Almost from the moment I applied to visit Mongolia, I was researching the best travel photography gear, camping gear, and more. Google Ads and Amazon made a lot of money off of me during those few months.

For most people, three to four months would be plenty of time to plan a trip to Asia. In fact, it turns out one of the last minute additions to the race had only a week to prepare. One week! I would not have slept for my racing brain.

And so I researched, read travel blogs, and generally made myself crazy. I packed a suitcase in June. Yes,

June! Then I unpacked it and bought a different suitcase. I would be traveling to Asia, basically camping, and doing it all for two weeks. How was a woman expected to do this and with photography equipment no less? I was in a tizzy. Plus, I had zero experience as a camper.

For months, I bought items I thought I'd need and piled them by the wall next to my bedroom window. I looked like a hoarder and it was slowly driving my husband crazy.

I'll be honest, I was going a little crazy as well. I would awaken in the night, wondering if everything would fit, or if the sleeping bag I bought would be sufficient.

What does one pack for a trip they know virtually nothing about? It's one thing to travel to Europe with the opportunity to buy new clothing or necessary items you forgot to include. But I would be in a country that does not speak English, in the city for a very limited time, and then in the middle of the desert. If I forgot something, I was out of luck.

And so the ping ponging in my brain continued. In a way, worrying about what I would bring to Mongolia kept me busy and away from thinking about leaving my family for two weeks.

I'm sure you are curious what I packed and whether

with all this careful thought I was happily successful. Yes, and no. I should have researched Beijing Airport, but even after traveling throughout the world, China was a surprise to me, and not in a good way. Little did I know that Beijing had a reputation, one which I learned firsthand. But you'll hear more about that later.

What are the basics a traveler should pack for a horse race in Mongolia?

The Gobi Desert Cup provides tents. It was mandatory I bring a sleeping pad, sleeping bag, one suitcase, a water bottle with purifier tablets for the non-potable water, comfortable shoes, my official Gobi Desert Cup shirts I'd purchased, undergarments, and socks.

There would be no running water in the desert and only basic accommodations, so as such I didn't plan on bringing much in the way of makeup or toiletries. I focused on the important things, a toothbrush, chapstick, moisturizer, and all-purpose Castile soap for hair and washing.

I did bring a few things I did not end up using. Well, a lot of things. And I forgot a lot of things, like a razor. One of the best things I brought on the recommendation of a travel blog is baby wipes. I didn't use many, but they helped to wipe the dirt and grime off as well as supplement a shower on days where we simply didn't have access to water.

Overall, I was really happy with my packing. I love to use compression sacks. I labeled each one: clothing, undergarments, socks, dirty clothes, protein bars, etc. Not only does it make packing into one piece of luggage easier, but I was able to find everything I needed even in the darkened ger with only a headlamp for limited lighting.

My suitcase was actually a genius move and my shining glory. I initially bought a collapsible and rolling duffel from Eagle Creek as my back up luggage. The plan was initially to pack it and bring back lots of goodies for myself and family from my adventures. However, with the wheels it took up a lot of room, even when it was collapsed. And I decided against a hard, rolling suitcase realizing that it would be easier for travel but not for fitting into a truck in the desert. So, I used the Eagle Creek rolling duffle bag. It was large and unwieldy but fit everything, including the 20 copies of *Confessions of a Timid Rider* I brought with me to the desert for the riders! It absolutely was so easy to pack with the compression bags, and I could even latch my sleeping bag onto the outside for ease while changing camps. The best part? I placed it on the outside of the ger, next to my sleeping mat to block the cool breeze and dirt from blowing in on me during the night.

Camille told me later that she was shocked I had never

camped before because I was so organized and looked like I knew what I was doing. Fake it until you make it!

I made two major mistakes. One, I brought only one iPhone charger. I know, I know rookie mistake. I thought I had more, but honestly, there was so much stuff! I realized while in the Beijing airport that my phone wasn't charging and my cord was broken. Fantastic. I mean, really? Not even 24 hours into my trip and I'm having issues – so much for all my careful planning!

Luckily, Mongolia is a group effort. I borrowed a charger from one of the riders, then basically commandeered a charging cord for the remainder of the event from one of the officials who didn't need it. I mean, my job was to keep the Facebook page updated so the public could follow the riders' progress and cheer them on! Not easy to do without a working phone. Thank goodness for her, honestly.

The second mistake was my camping mat.

It sucked.

I did my research, but I didn't have several hundred dollars to spend on a product I may only use once. The biggest piece of advice I can give to you is that you get what you pay for. It's a cliché for a reason!

One thing you should know about The Gobi Desert Cup

is that the basecamp changes every few days as riders travel the course. Basecamp and training are two days, and then everyone packs up everything like a nomad, (that is the point), and moves to a new camp. There we may stay only one night, or perhaps more. So we must be organized and pack up everything before breakfast on moving days. My sleeping pad was inflatable and easily compressed, but it would squeak every time I sat or moved on it. It became worse throughout the event and it was so embarrassing!

One evening at dinner I wore a tank top as we were in the southern end of the Gobi more than halfway through the course. Everyone was asking if I was okay, and I had no idea why. There are no mirrors anywhere, so I had no idea that my arms and back were covered in small bruises. It probably looked like I was manhandled. Alas, it was for a much more mundane reason. My sleeping pad had a hole somewhere. After three days, I would wake up each morning on the ground. Luckily, I was so tired from working all day in the fresh air that I still slept. I'm a very light sleeper at home, and this is one of the reasons I was always hesitant to camp.

But in the desert, it's really hard to locate and fix a small hole in your sleeping pad. From dawn to dark, I was working. The only lights in the ger were limited and dim, usually as a result of a headlamp. I just kept inflating the mattress pad and hoping for at least a modicum of comfort. It was a big mistake not to invest in a large and more functional sleep pad. I slept on the ground for the last few days, without any cushioning at all.

So, my advice is this, do your research. Invest your money in a good quality product and company. Trust me, if you work with a highly respected company and your product fails on you, they will likely replace it for free. I wasted a lot of money on items that I didn't need or that didn't work.

Do you want to know my favorite and most used travel item?

A multifunction folding knife with LED light. This item I kept on me at all times. Not only did I use it daily, but the other officials and riders borrowed it to either tighten fenders, open wine or beer, or trim something. My biggest fear was not getting it back because it was borrowed so often!

I have traveled my whole life. I love traveling to new countries and experiencing other cultures. My father was a Captain in the Air Force, flying in Vietnam, and when he retired he worked for many years in the aviation insurance industry. This resulted in a lot of travel for my father and stories he brought home, often with gifts from faraway lands. My sister and I flew by ourselves when I was about nine or ten to meet our parents in Virginia. It was a short flight, and easy enough.

Over the years, we drove or flew to most of the Continental United States and throughout Europe and the United Kingdom. Often, traveling was chaotic, but also fun and adventurous. When I met my husband, I was shocked to realize that he had never ventured very far from home.

After traveling to Australia, which was exhausting but worth it, I knew that I could handle a 13-hour flight to Beijing easily. After all, it was only two hours from there to Ulaanbataar in Mongolia.

Jinxed myself, didn't I? Like in the Greek myths, hubris will always be a downfall, and I was so proud of my travel experience. But I wasn't ready for China.

The flight to Beijing was simple, textbook in fact, other than a little restless leg syndrome. I confess that I underestimated many things. For example, the different time zones, the language barrier, the sheer amount of photography equipment to be scanned by security, and my jet lag.

I traveled with Canadian natural horsemanship trainer, Lorie, who was leaving North America for the first time, and we were both excited for our adventure. Deplaning was simple and we had one hour and forty minutes until our connecting flight. While Lorie had a boarding pass for the connection, United Airways did not give me one for Air China. As such, we had to leave the gated area and travel to the desk for Air China where I was able to ask for my boarding pass through a mixture of English and hand charades.

Logistics done, we found the International Connections area and traveled through, but my passport would not scan! Holding up the line behind me, with Lorie already through and waiting in the security checkpoint, I needed assistance from a guard. Luckily my passport worked with help and my photo was taken. Off I traveled to security!

Woo hoo!

Security screening is never anyone's favorite. There is always some character who forgets to take off his or her shoes, or remove their liquids, and holds up the line.

That was me.

With all my travel experience, I thought I had seen it all when it came to security. Oh, how wrong I was. I was traveling with an exceptional amount of electronic equipment and spare batteries in my arsenal. GoPro had sponsored six Hero 6 cameras with accessories that I was hauling to Mongolia. In addition, I had my laptop computer, tablet, phone, and Nikon with multiple lenses and back-up batteries. This accounted for most of my carry-on luggage. I had no idea that Beijing would be so strict with their guidelines.

The first time I went through security, I removed the major electronics as well as my camera. But no, I needed to remove every single GoPro, every battery, every lens, EVERYTHING. Coupled with my boots and jacket I had almost five bins to run through the scanner. Of course, I was pat down by the guards, and pulled to the side to go through my items where, to my horror, I saw that many things were being confiscated one by one. Goodbye solar charger, and not one, but two, back-up portable phone chargers. I nearly cried right there. The batteries were too powerful to be carried on, but could not be stowed, so I was not allowed to have them at all. All my research, shopping, and planning for months on just the right things to bring, out the window and probably to be sold on the black market.

It must have taken 45 minutes to an hour before I got through security. I was sweating. Between struggling not to cry, unpacking everything, repacking everything (badly), I was exhausted and defeated. I needed a glass of wine.

I didn't see Lorie anywhere, so she probably got tired of waiting for me. When I exited, sweating and exhausted, I found her by the gate directory and we decided to check our gate and see if the plane was there, assuming we still had plenty of time. After all, we'd had almost two hours before our connecting flight was supposed to leave. Plenty of time, even with the delay in security.

We arrived at the gate, but there is no one there. No one was sitting waiting for their flight, no airline worker at the gate, no plane. Okay no problem. Lorie and I assumed we are too early. This is China and maybe they run things differently.

We decided to grab a glass of wine next to the gate and waited for the announcer to call for boarding. It seemed so simple at the time. After all, I travel frequently and knew what I was doing.

After 30 minutes or so I got nervous, so we rushed to pay the bill and headed to the gate. Except there still wasn't any one there. No plane, no people, no gate attendant. I checked the board, but the flight wasn't listed.

What the hell happened?

We were baffled. We were right next to the gate with no indications the plane had been and gone. And according to our watches, we were on time! Even our smartphones had automatically updated to the appropriate time zone.

In a panic, Lorie and I dragged all our carry-on luggage with us, running through the terminal looking for someone, anyone, who spoke English. Finally, we accosted a young pilot for Air China and asked him whether we missed our flight. My companion turned on the charm, and I sat silent because I know what he was going to say…we were stranded. But while I can admit the truth to myself, Lorie refused to give up. We raced throughout the terminal, desperate to find someone to help us and hoping instead they moved our gate without announcing it on the directory.

We must have spoken to four pilots as we raced along. Every time we found an employee who would shake their head "no" and point us in another direction. This response was so prevalent it became an inside joke for us later on when we could breathe again.

Finally, we admitted defeat. There were only two flights per day from Beijing to Ulaanbataar, Mongolia, and we had missed them both. Covered in sweat and fifteen hours of travel dust, we went back to the Air China counter to change our tickets for the next possible flight out, which would be 18 hours later.

The Disappointments Keep Coming

Perhaps my expectations were too high. My experience so far in China was far beneath what I had anticipated. There was no staff at the gate, no speaker announcements, and very strict security guidelines. But we couldn't dwell on our missed flight. We had an adventure race to get to and only limited time!

Off we hustled to find our way back to the ticket booth.

Only there were no exits. Zero, zip, zilch. Seriously, there was no legal way for us to go back through to the ticket counter. The only way out was on a flight. Somehow, and I'm still grateful, we talked our way behind security with two male security guards. We traveled up the stairs, lugging our baggage, and knocked at the private security gate for another guard to let us out. They did not want to and called another person over. We explained as best we could our situation despite the language barrier. Finally, after much prodding, they allowed us out.

With hearts in our throats, two hours after we were last at the Air China ticket counter, we returned.

I know that Americans assume everyone will speak English, but if you think that then you are absolutely incorrect. I knew it and had traveled throughout European countrysides successfully with halting French, Italian, or Dutch and the use of charades. But China, specifically Beijing, is an altogether different beast. There, five men and women stared at us as if we were mythical dragons in life, not understanding why we had boarding passes and wanted new ones. Finally, our message got across and they crushed us with their message.

The Air China counter does not issue tickets.

Never in my life had I been to an airport where the

airline counter did not book or reschedule flights. Without a Chinese SIM card, we were expected to call Air China on the phone and book our new tickets. The counter employees were unwilling to do even that for us. So here we were, expected to phone an airline for new tickets in a language we didn't know while standing in front of their local airport branch. The mind boggles.

I thought Lorie was going to lose it right there, and I kept imagining ending up in a foreign prison. I've seen Bridget Jones, so while she begged and argued and tried to rationalize with these people while trying to reach her own travel agent by phone, I moved aside trying to get internet access to Expedia.

After probably 45 minutes to an hour, but what felt like longer, I was able to book two tickets on Expedia from Beijing to Ulaanbataar for the next morning. We were so relieved! Finally, things were going right for us, even if I had to purchase two more tickets and spend money I didn't have.

With our new boarding passes in hand, we once again went through the gauntlet of passport customs and security screening. My photo was already in the system, so it didn't want to let me through, but finally I got the green light. Security, I expected to remain a challenge and it was; however, now I knew how strict they were and there wasn't a huge line or a looming flight to catch adding extra pressure.

One problem solved. Now the question was where would we sleep?

The very helpful (not) Air China employees suggested a hotel outside the airport, but we lacked visas because we were supposed to be traveling straight through to Mongolia. There was a suggestion of a travel visa for these very scenarios, but honestly, I wasn't willing to risk it. I did not have much faith in Beijing or China thus far in my experience. We didn't find out until much later as we were leaving that there was an hourly hotel in the airport terminal.

So off we ventured to eat something horrible in the airport and take a few silly photos in the beautiful pagodas in the center of the terminal. Make the best of a terrible situation, right?

Exhaustion finally overcame us, and we decided to plant ourselves at our original gate to sleep if we could.

I slept with my arm wrapped around my luggage, protecting my equipment. Photo courtesy of ©Lorie Duff.

Even that was an adventure!

Picture this. A very tired and hungry woman from New Jersey who hates being late for anything and is a light sleeper as a result of having three children. Are you picturing it? Now imagine she is carrying about $4,000-$5,000 worth of electronic equipment and is relegated to sleeping in the same clothes she's been wearing for 18 hours, in public.

This sounds like the makings of a terrible monster from a horror movie. I was the hangry, smelly rage monster.

I dozed a few minutes here or there, always with my hand, (and sometimes arm), through my luggage. You can take the girl out of New Jersey, but you can't make her trust anyone.

Eventually I had to use the restroom and since Lorie appeared to be sleeping, I quietly brought my luggage with me not wanting to disturb her. Halfway to the long walk to use the facilities I realized that I left my phone behind. But my bladder wasn't waiting. I rushed back to find my phone gone, picked up in Lorie's frantic hands thinking I'd been kidnapped!

Who can blame her? My phone was always in my hand and I would never, ever leave it behind willingly. Thankfully, I wasn't kidnapped although I did give her a heart attack.

Hard to sleep after that but we had fits and starts. Eventually she was able to reach her travel agent who was trying to have the airline reissue our tickets at no extra charge. In the wee hours of the morning, while the rest of Beijing slept, we received the first good news. Her agent was able to get the tickets reissued and sent us the new confirmation numbers. All we had to do was reissue the boarding pass. Yes, you read that part correctly. We needed a third boarding pass, and I wanted to die.

For the third time, we needed to visit the Air China counter. We could only hope that this was our lucky break and it was staffed. The airport was deadly quiet, but almost comforting in a way. I'm not sure why I felt that way considering the experience, but dare I say it was becoming familiar? After all we had been living there for an entire day.

So, we traveled back past the security guards, up the familiar hallway behind the scenes to the secret "not exit" for their TSA that we had used earlier, schlepping our luggage once again. Yet this time, no amount of pleading could persuade the waiting guard to allow us to exit with her security pass to visit the Air China counter, tantalizingly within sight just ahead. With military strictness, she turned us around and made us return the way we had come. Only we couldn't.

Entry was one way, and we had to travel yet through another secret security hallway to another entrance to the terminal. Can you guess where it took us? We had to travel back through SECURITY. For the third time, I unpacked each of my electronics for the waiting guards and scanning machines. Only now the morning travelers were starting to arrive en masse, and it was getting crowded.

You know the saying, third time's the charm? This is not the case with Beijing security. To say I was over it is an understatement of epic proportions. It was crowded, I was incredibly dirty, hadn't slept in about 30 hours, and was incredibly cranky. With a big sigh, I submitted to full body scanning, a pat down, emptied my bag of electronics, repacked my bag with electronics, and tried to find our new gate.

Then, in the distance, a blessing appeared on the horizon in the form of Starbucks.

I could have cried. Maybe I did shed a discreet tear or two. But there it was like a beacon of hope for our exit out of the damned Beijing airport.

And with my drink and a blueberry muffin in hand, I had the strength to power through the remaining two hours before our flight. We perched at the gate and refused to leave.

Without our new boarding passes I was hesitant to cancel my Expedia tickets. There was no guarantee that we would talk our way onto the flight, and once again there was no gate attendant in sight.

Finally, about 15 minutes before the flight, the gate attendant arrived, and Lorie went to work to get our new boarding passes. I'd like to tell you that as the sun rose in the East and lit up the airport, revealing the plane waiting for us at the gate, that we printed our boarding passes, boarded the plane, and left China without a backward glance. Sadly, it didn't quite work out like that. Lorie was able to persuade the gate attendant to call her supervisor who thankfully spoke English and get a verbal agreement to board the plane for only her ticket. They couldn't issue a new boarding pass! So as the last few people boarded, (it was the quickest I've ever seen), they quickly wrote down the new number on her old boarding pass and just waved her on.

I tried to pull up enough internet connection to cancel the Expedia flight, which was well within the 24 hours, but it just wouldn't work. Determined to get on the plane and travel to Mongolia, I put down my phone and enjoyed the ride.

The relief I felt finally arriving in Ulanbaatar was an understatement. I'm not sure what I was expecting from the capital of Mongolia, but the small airport wasn't it. Afterward, I realized this was quite biased of me, especially after living in Beijing for 20 hours. It was easy to find the baggage claim despite the language barrier. I just followed the flow of traffic toward the exit.

My fear was that we wouldn't find out luggage, which should have arrived 24 hours before. What if my bag was lost, or worse, stolen? All the careful planning and packing that I worried over would be for nothing. My traveling companion found her bag on the conveyor belt quickly, which gave me hope! I stood there, biting my nails both exhausted and smelly, only wanting a shower and something to eat. Finally, there it was! My bag was wrapped in cellophane, so I didn't recognize at first, but it was there, and the lock was on it. Phew!

I breathed a huge sigh of relief. Luckily, it had already

been scanned so we were able to walk straight though and get our customs stamp. Only then did we realize that the currency exchange was upstairs, and we'd have to go back through customs lugging all of our gear. I was so done. Near the exit I saw the driver with a sign for our hotel, and that clinched it for me.

Honestly, I probably would have left with anyone that day if they'd offered me hot water and a meal. Luckily, I had messaged Camille, and she told the hotel we were arriving on a different flight. We were also traveling with two other recent arrivals, including Scandinavian Jon who would be riding with us in the event. Success!

It was a fun ride to the city center. While we shared travel stories with each other and short introductions, I gazed out the window to the pale grey skies and low mountains surrounding the city on one side, to the other filled with small huts and buildings.

7

FIRST IMPRESSIONS

My first impression of Ulanbaatar was *dust*. I don't want to say dirty, because despite being a city, this is a country very much tied to nature and only a small portion is roads. I expected dirt. I mean "dusty" because every time we would slow to a stop, I would turn to watch someone taking a rag and wiping down their dashboards. Without vehicle air conditioning, the windows were open, and dust seeped in and coated everything. I did not realize at the time that the city is incredibly polluted, especially in winter due to the burning of coal to keep warm. The air quality is low, and what I took for dark clouds were perhaps not clouds at all.

I remember thinking to myself, "What have I gotten myself into?" While I knew this was a third-world country I did not see the beauty of the city right away. This came much later once I took the time to stop, look around, and appreciate its beauty.

The biggest impression I learned from my first car ride, and was only accentuated the next day, is that Mongolian drivers have very few rules and are afraid of NOTHING.

I cannot stress this enough. The hotel driver was on his best behavior for us but had to stop constantly because of four-way traffic. Bikes and cars would creep out from a 90 degree angle, aggressively inserting themselves so we would be forced to stop abruptly to let them pass. Multiple cars struggled to move in separate directions without traffic lights, stop signs, or police directing traffic. It was chaos but yet somehow worked, because we made it to the hotel unscathed albeit a little delayed.

The hotel itself was much grander than I had anticipated. I immediately soaked myself in the bathtub, lathering up with fragrant soap and hot water to rinse myself of my travels before changing and heading downstairs to the restaurant. It felt odd to be alone in another country, but new experiences like this fuel me, (as long as I'm not in the saddle).

As I hovered near the entrance to the restaurant, I spied a familiar face from the website and photos… it was

Camille! She saw me at the same time and came to greet me, inviting me to sit with her and the others. Into the fire I went! I had had limited to no contact with these women, but I felt immediately connected by our mutual excitement.

So there I sat, perfectly on time, (for once this trip), to order lunch and get to know Camille Champagne, Dr. Ann Lammens, and our Steward, Colleen. Later, Rosie Barr, a teacher from New Zealand and friend of Camille's, arrived. She attended last minute to help assist the Ride Director and be a general helper where she was most needed. Over Spaghetti Carbonara, (a welcome treat), we exchanged stories and learned a little more about each other while preparing for the event the next morning. I can only imagine the first impression that I made. I was likely a bit relieved to arrive and a bit manic as well, but Camille told me her impression was that she thought I'd be a bit taller.

Ha!

Like I've never heard that before. I stand at 5'0" tall but with a whole lot of personality.

It's not easy being the new kid on the block, and I was completely out of my comfort zone. Not only was I joining the officials, (luckily there were a few other newbies as well), but I was in a country I didn't know with an event I'd only ever read about. But I was finally here.

Talk about taking a risk!

The Riders

Meeting the riders was interesting, and one of those surreal moments. I'd interacted with most of them in advance of the event, even interviewing some, and traveling with another. But to see all 18 riders together, getting to know each other, and excited, but nervous, for the race, was so inspiring. Here I was, technically an official, but learning for the first time.

I noticed quickly that riders grouped themselves together, but the effect wasn't a clique in any way. Everyone was inclusive but gravitated toward those with whom they felt most comfortable. It was amazing.

I generally feel more comfortable with animals than humans. Often, I'm underwhelmed by humans' capacity for drama and self-importance. While it's my job in many ways to be on social media, it often showcases the best and worst of human nature. With only 48 hours away from the rest of the world, I viewed a small microcosm of society uniting based on a mutual love of adventure and horses. We were all there with the goal to experience Mongolia through the eyes of a nomad.

After our group breakfast it was like herding cats to load the riders and their gear in the trucks. The riders didn't want to sit in the vans and wait, so we couldn't load the trucks with their luggage, and so forth. This became a case of who would I like to sit with? The first loading was difficult but was much easier after the fact, and it helped that we continued to take roll call to make sure no man or woman was left behind.

Then, finally, we were off!

The Drivers

I mentioned before about Mongolian drivers. I learned a few things very quickly.

- Where are the seat belts?
- Roads are optional.

- Drivers do not break for wandering animals.
- The roofs are cushioned for a reason.

ON THE OUTSKIRTS OF UB, AS WE CALLED THE CAPITAL, narrow two-lane roads lead past the iconic Genghis Khan statue and out toward the country. There are road stands, gers, and many livestock. If you want to go faster than the car in front of you, drivers accelerate alarmingly to pass, often driving on both lanes of traffic like a giant game of chicken. At one point, our driver was so determined to pass a car and traveled onto the dirt track, almost hitting a cement barrier that loomed suddenly in front of us. I breathed a sigh of relief when we reached the open dirt tracks. That is, until the drivers decided to compete with each other again and race in their own version of the Mongol Rally.

While many riders enjoyed the flinging and bouncing, it was too much for me. My camera equipment was in danger of breaking, and at some point, I thought we would tip over.

Traveling on Mongolian roads.

Roads in Mongolia are little more than dirt tracks. Where the tracks are well-traveled and riddled with holes, the drivers go off course and make their own way. These trucks in general are Russian lorries built in the 1970s without much in the way of shock absorbers.

Finally, we pulled the driver over and asked them all to stop with their behavior. While they may have been having fun, not everyone else was.

Every pit stop is a photo op!

I learned very quickly that these drivers take risks, don't believe in rules, and have a serious competitive streak. Basically, all things that go against my very nature. I was so out of my comfort zone – 6,336 miles outside of my comfort zone if I want to be literal.

8

A BREEZY TOUR ACROSS THE COUNTRYSIDE

That first drive to basecamp was an adventure all on its own. Everything so far had been an adventure and the race had not yet begun. The drivers somehow felt we were joining the Mongol Rally and raced each other, using dirt tracks, avoiding rocks and holes with sudden swerves. I learned quickly why the lorries had cushioned ceilings.

Most of the riders enjoyed every minute, but we had a few older officials and riders, and frankly, it got old. I'm all for a little fun here or there, but I didn't want to roll or die before we'd arrived at the basecamp. To finally arrive but plan and prepare all these months for nothing? No way was I willing to let that happen.

We had a serious conversation with the drivers, whose fun was ruined, and they began to drive at a better pace. With calmer, but still aggressive maneuvers typical of Mongolia, we toured the vast countryside through different provinces several hours to reach our basecamp.

With word from camp indicating the tents were wet from the evening rain, we needed to delay slightly and took an unexpected stop to visit a 13th century ger, similar to what Genghis Khan would have wintered in. I only wish we were able to take photos without a fee, but it was huge and the attention to detail impeccable with gold painted into the wooden designs.

My fingers were itching on the camera with so many visual delights. Even at modest speed, the trucks bumped and bounced along, maneuvering to avoid sharp rocks or dips. As such, my sensitive Nikon stayed preciously in my lap, unable to focus well on the moving targets and yet too delicate for me to try and put back in the bag without accidentally snapping it. My iPhone instead became a tool that I relied on, capturing video and images that I still look at periodically and remember fondly.

Even from my first moments on the adventure I had to put aside my best laid plans and adjust accordingly. In life, I'm a planner. While I am decisive, I am not usually spontaneous in any way. Everything is well thought out with pros and cons balanced as needed. But Mongolia immediately tested my comfort zone and pushed me out of it.

Camille warned me before the event that, "Some people face physical tests and others mental. But everyone learns something about themselves." She was so right. My journey to self-enlightenment was just beginning and the race hadn't yet started.

It is not just the riders who are tested.

We took the circuitous route and took a long pit stop near the river. Mongolia is a beautiful land, named the "Land of Eternal Blue Sky" for good reason. However, water is precious and not readily available. The nomads must move their livestock to find good grazing and water supplies, which are affected by drought and sometimes disease. The riders were grateful to stretch their legs and have a quick snack or use the "toilet," which you can imagine is basically anywhere on the ground, preferably with a little distance from the group. Little did they know they would become quite comfortable urinating in front of others after a few days. There is very little coverage to hide behind. Scratch that, no coverage.

Many of us went to inspect the water's edge and photograph the feral horses seeking shade underneath the bridge. It smelled of horse, but also that much heavier smell of cow pie, drifting pungently across the narrow water. The flies were prevalent and when the stray dogs came to say hello, they were covered in nits and other parasites.

We had been warned that most dogs are unfriendly and often are used to guard flocks against wolves. I met quite a few dogs on my trek, and I was fascinated by their friendliness and lack of guardedness. All animals in Mongolia serve a purpose. And while the nomads may respect and even feel affection for some of them, they are not pets as they live feral and take their guard duties seriously.

Some of the more adventurous riders crouched down for belly rubs and earned some affection from our four-legged friends. I felt bad for the mangled fur and eyes covered in insect eggs. These are not the prized show animals or pampered pooches you see in New Jersey. My heart ached for them, and yet they exuded so much love and openness that I couldn't help but be inspired by their generous hearts. Still, I was unwilling to pet them with my hands and used my foot. Better safe than sorry as I doubted baby wipes would help remove a parasite.

Soon after the riders' patience wore thin, practically frothing at the mouth to get to basecamp and get on a horse. With a few other stops to fix a flat tire and pass a police checkpoint, our parade of Russian lorries finally crested the horizon to view our base camp on the horizon. We had spent an entire day traveling to our destination.

Basecamp was the start of everything. The riders had their eye on the prize and were excited to meet the horses and begin their adventure.

The drive had been riddled with flat tires, pit stops, excitement, and then frustration. If I learned anything from my driven tour across that vast land is that anything can happen and probably will. You have to be prepared for anything, expect nothing, and go with the flow. Because there is a reason for everything, even when you cannot understand it at the time.

The breezy tour across inner Mongolia had come to an

end. While I'd begun capturing what I could on film and video, the rocky terrain and lack of shocks on the trucks prevented use of my sensitive Nikon. This was my first time, and I was as wide-eyed and eager for the experience as the riders.

9

HITTING THE GROUND RUNNING

Upon arriving at basecamp, it was time to hit the ground running. Camille immediately asked for photos of the camp before the riders came in, and I was off like a shot. I followed her, wanting to capture her greeting her partner, Nara, and the herders she knew from the year before. I left my bags at the trucks and took off as fast as I could move. (For the record, it's not very fast. Just in case you were wondering).

The trouble with photographing an event of this magnitude is being everywhere at once. There were so many things to capture and it was daunting. More, as it was my first time, I didn't know what to prioritize. I was grateful but determined to succeed and very

Top left to right: Rosie Barr, Dr. Ian Baines, Dr. Ann Lammens. Bottom left to right: Camille Champagne, Heather Wallace, Dr. Julie Kemp.

overwhelmed. Luckily, I had help from Julie, an Australian who came as my assistant photographer and doubled as the on-course veterinarian. Once I got my bearings, I was able to delegate and prioritize.

Still, I would change a few things going forward, different angles and capturing shots that I didn't think to photograph earlier.

I tend to be an overachiever, and what's more, I had something to prove. I wanted Camille and her team to know they made the right decision bringing me on board, all the way across the world. I knew I could do the job, but it certainly was a big one.

How could one person fully capture a 10-day endurance horse race in Mongolia, provide regular social media posts without a strong Wi-Fi signal, interview every single rider, and more?

I'm sweating just thinking how I managed to do it.

I worked hard from the moment we arrived. The stress to perform sent me running for the camp toilet that first night, hoping I wouldn't crap my pants before I reached the distant tent. I made it, barely, and that was the last time I would defecate for the rest of the time there. I just didn't have the time and energy to spare. Plus, on the second day of toilet use, the tents became riddled with flies and smelled awful. We learned by the end of the week to only use each toilet for a single day.

Enough potty talk though.

I struggled, but happily so, with capturing everything I could and also having the opportunity to experience it myself as a participant and not just an observer. It's a delicate balance, but one I believe I accomplished.

Basecamp on Day One: Horse Line and a Rider's Tent

The first few days at basecamp there was zero phone or internet service, making posting updates for loved ones back home on the event FB page impossible. I had some great footage and updates and no one to share them with! While this was a great opportunity for riders to unplug, my job was to make sure everyone at home knew what we were doing and that their family members and friends were safe and having fun. I knew they were probably worried because they hadn't received an update.

The first race day, the course took us through a small village. I didn't feel comfortable with my own truck and rode with Camille and her driver.

We drove around slowly, looking for the best signal, and then pulled over. It was hot, so incredibly hot, but dry and with a breeze. There is no air-conditioning in the vehicles, so we left the windows open and the driver stepped out for some air and a cigarette.

I had a whole slew of posts to send out. Text-only posts take very little bandwidth, and photos were a little slow to load. But I learned the hard way that a one-minute video interview with a rider would be the most frustrating thing. Video became my nemesis. It took me over 40 minutes to *almost* load the file before it would crash out on me, causing me to growl in frustration. All the while, Camille sat calmly by trying to reach her husband and baby at home or coordinate with the herders and other officials on course.

Eventually, we figured it out. Every time we would drive through a town, I would take the drafts and quickly publish them all, one-by-one, so they wouldn't time out and freeze the system. I was even able to post a few videos sparingly, and only under the watchful eye of the Wi-Fi booster provided in my ger each evening.

Providing water for horses at the 40km hold.
Everyone pitches in what they can.

There was no real downtime. Before and during the event I was photographing, jotting down notes, helping at checkpoints, or capturing what I could on video. Returning to camp, I was compiling social media posts, editing videos, or coercing the riders to do a sit-down interview with me. Most were nervous to be on camera, so instead of talking at them, I chose to sit with them and ask fellow official and general awesome girl, Rosie Roo, to be my camera woman.

By the time dinner rolled around, I was spent. I didn't want to shower in the dark, so I went days with just baby wipes to remove the sweat until I couldn't stand it any longer.

A few nights I needed to collapse in the ger. Some nights I needed to blow off some steam.

On our way to our last basecamp of the race, we had a two-hour drive. The riders were exhausted having ridden that day and didn't realize we were transporting them from the finish line to our final camp site. The day was incredibly hot, perhaps the hottest yet. We ended at a large pond, and some of the riders "strapped" or cooled their horses in it, letting them roll and play. More, we were greeted by the Buddhist Lama (monk) that had blessed our event on the first race day, and he brought friends with him!

Our final camp would be near a monastery and we were honored they supported our event and encouraged our work with the locals and their horses.

It took us forever to all be ready to go to our next camp. We were hot, tired, and ready to just have some quiet time. Finally, horses were transported, we herded the hot and tired riders on their trucks, and everyone got gasoline. Camille decided to make an extra stop. She had a feeling and she was right – we all needed to let loose some steam. Appearing like an angel in the distance, she handed out bottles of wine and warm beer to each truck for the long ride.

But we had the best truck. Camille and Rosie are the best of friends, and I loved them both, although I was acutely aware that I was there because of Camille and wanted to impress her. So, while I'd spent a lot of time with Rosie, joking and laughing, I was definitely more serious with the Ride Director. I was intimidated. I'll happily admit it.

But that ride to camp changed something. Yes, warm beer has a way of doing that, but I actually let myself relax. I don't know if I've ever laughed so much in my life. Our driver played music and we plugged in our phones, singing along to Katy Perry and Eminem. The latter threw us over the edge. With Gobi Desert Cup hats twisted to the side to look like rappers, (except we just looked silly), we struggled to rap to "Shady's Back" and kept messing up. I even tried to get it on video and then realized I forgot to press record, (something that was a recurring theme), and then laughed hysterically at that. We tried to get the mojo back on camera, but it didn't work. Which of course was even more entertaining to us all as we dissolved into fits and giggles.

The clincher was singing "I Kissed a Girl" at the top of our lungs and looking over to see our driver smirking. Apparently, he'd opened up his radio so all the other drivers and riders could hear us without us knowing. We arrived at camp in great spirits to find all the riders laughing at us good-naturedly.

That evening we were all happy. It was our last camp, and we knew the end was in sight. There may have been dancing, and there may have been a conversation between the Lama and myself on whether he liked Katy Perry or Pink best, and I played their music on my phone for him to decide, (for the record, Pink). I almost got him to dance as well, his idea, before Nara took him away for some "man" time in the nomad camp.

Perhaps I let my guard down a little too much.

I regret nothing and am incredibly proud of the work I did. Looking back, I would do things differently having experienced it and knowing what those at home want to know and riders want to see when they can get a glimpse of service. Just a few tweaks that would help me focus on certain aspects and better manage my time. I was a one-woman media monster with my Nikon and 200 mm lens harnessed over my shoulder, an iPhone in my hand for video interviews and photos for social media, and a GoPro strapped to my ball cap.

I'll still run around like a crazy person, taking a break to sit whenever possible and forgetting to eat something, but I will make more effort to relax with my fellow officials and take some down time.

10

THE MONGOLIAN HORSE

My first impression of a Mongolian horse was nothing like I'd expected.

I'd done my research. I'd watched films, and I scoured the internet to find out more about this unique breed of equine, whose DNA has remained unchanged for thousands of years. With export illegal, they are perhaps the last ancient horse remaining on the planet.

Equines easily outnumber the population of people in Mongolia 3-to-1 with an estimated three million horses in the country. It is not uncommon to see bands of horses wandering the steppe, an ecoregion of grassland plains. While horses first appeared in North America, they were arguably first domesticated in Central Asia by 5,000 BC. But there was no direct evidence of importance until the late Bronze Age around 1400 BC, shown by the ceremonial burial of several horses. Regardless, this species is incredibly important to their culture and the respect is apparent once stepping foot in the country. Horses in art, statues, and roaming the roads are prevalent.

Their proud ancestor Genghis Khan, after all, conquered most of Asia into Europe and the Middle East using the horse as his favorite weapon and source of transportation.

Appearance

Their ancient lines can be spotted in the zebra stripes on some of their legs, or the dorsal stripe appearing on some of their backs. They can be any color from grulla, or blue dun, to spotted like an Appaloosa. There are virtually no limits.

There are many things that make these animals unique. They are small, averaging perhaps between 12 and 14 hands but with large heads and compact bodies with short legs. Don't let their small stature fool you though; these horses are extremely tough.

Someone mentioned that their ribcages are triangular in shape instead of rounded like modern horses, but I could not find anything scientific to support that theory. Perhaps it is a modern myth or a tale told around the campfires in Mongolia.

Gender Norms

The nomads have very specific roles for their animals. Mares are revered and remain unridden, respected as mothers and a source of life. More, fermented grey mare's milk (airag) is a delicacy favored by many for feasts, by men and women, young and old. It is very strong in both smell and, I assume, taste. I am lactose intolerant and, frankly, the smell put me off. I was unwilling to risk unpasteurized milk products on my first evening at camp.

However, the locals swear by its nourishing properties and will advise that it may cure illnesses affecting the heart and lung, stomach, back, and rheumatism in addition to improving the metabolism.

Stallions are the pride of the herd and used for their favorite pastime, horse racing, which is one of the "three games of men" and celebrated by all at Naadam and many other races, with children competing on stallions for money and bragging rights. Thousands of horses may enter a race at any given time, and they are usually 20 kilometers in length.

Naturally, these horses have excellent endurance making them the perfect horse to ride for miles across the desert. Stallions' manes are kept long and drawn back for racing by colored bands to keep their eyes clear. The same is done at the base of the tails to keep the hair from slowing the horse around the hind legs.

Geldings, on the other hand, are prevalent and their manes and forelocks are cropped.

A typical Mongolian herd may consist of 15 – 50 mares

and geldings under one stallion. With over three million horses in Mongolia, it is apparent how important they are to the culture and given their due respect.

This year the Gobi Desert Cup had about 130 geldings trained, fed, and conditioned for the race. These horses are not used in traditional racing and thus result in an extra source of income for the nomads.

Wild or Semi-Feral?

There is a big difference between wild and feral. Wild denotes natural and untamed, whereas feral means domesticated but living wild, such is the Mongolian horse. There are no fences in this vast country. By day the horses may wander in a herd or wait for work on a traditional horse line. By night, the horses roam free and may move great distances, on average 10 kilometers, in search of grass and water. Each morning the herdsmen will wake before dawn to muster their horses, often bringing them in tied to each other, one nomad with six to eight horses in tow.

Living feral has several repercussions. The horses are leaner than their modern, Western counterparts. It is not uncommon to view their ribs and even hips as they subsist only on whatever grass they can find. More, they tend to be covered in cuts and scratches that leave scars due to lack of veterinary access and resulting natural healing. Additionally, their hooves are barefoot and untrimmed, naturally filed down by digging for roots and roaming large distances.

Wild horses are unrideable until they are trained and acclimated to humans. The Mongolian horses are already used to being ridden but live wild and free.

Temperament

This breed is known for their docile nature. Many of us would be surprised at our own horses not being ridden for months and then one day, pulled out of the herd, saddled, and requested to work. And yet, these horses do.

I had always assumed that the horses would be fully wild. When I told friends and family I was working for an endurance horse race in Mongolia, everyone assumed it was the Mongol Derby and tried to warn me off. In fact, I did watch *All the Wild Horses*, the fascinating film by Ivo Marloh about the Derby, in advance of the trip. I thoroughly enjoyed the film; however, I wondered if I had bitten off more than I could chew. The horses for the MD were pulled from local herders willing to offer them up for rent to their riders without any prior training or conditioning for the Western riders. I watched as horses kicked, spun, reared, and bucked, resulting in injury after injury to both horses and riders.

But this is not the norm for the Gobi Desert Cup. Yes, these horses are more feral than the horses we are used to, but much of it has to do with the approach and connection. The nomads are fearless, no nonsense, and unflappable.

At basecamp we had the pleasure of watching the herders demonstrate their horsemanship skills. I've never seen such calm. The only emotion from the men was a sense of fun and pride. They first drove horses into a temporary round pen, culling the colt they wanted to ride with a long stick and rope attachment. Once pulled, the scared horse was driven to its knees to allow the rider on its back. Once he was on, the rope was removed and there was the nomad, bridle-less, bareback, and with no fences. He would use a hat or hand to encourage the horse to buck and kick, tiring him before galloping off into the distance. I worried, but soon he would turn back with a tired horse, fully connected and now rideable.

The entire process perhaps took 30 minutes to an hour.

Perhaps it is herd living that keeps these horses so happy and calm when under saddle. The trick is to learn who their friends are, and often they will ride together very well. Get a Mongolian horse on its own, and if you don't have a good connection, that horse will likely walk the whole way.

While I initially felt nerves, I quickly came to realize that my assumptions of Mongolian horses were incorrect. Yes, they can certainly buck and spin, all horses are capable of that behavior. However, they are much more willing and docile than I anticipated.

What I noticed most was how important confidence and connection is with these horses. Lack of confidence may incite natural prey behavior; however, a calm connection and quiet communication is extremely effective. The nomads make it look effortless; you could hardly see them using their aids. Once, when riding a performance barrel horse, someone told me to just think "walk." I scoffed at first. Yet, I've seen it work. More, I've felt it myself.

11

ON THE OUTSIDE LOOKING IN

The Big Race

All this build up and all this anticipation and the centerpiece of it all is the race itself. I had zero experience with endurance riding. While New Jersey is riddled with horse farms and green space, the wide open expanses of the western United States provides more fertile ground for these 50 mile and 100 mile events. All I knew were the local hunter paces, approximately 8 miles, and I hadn't even worked up the courage to do one of those!

As you can imagine, The Gobi Desert Cup was a learning experience in many ways. The premise is 480 kilometers, about 300 miles, in a multistage event over six days. Approximately 50 miles per day each on a different Mongolian horse. Arabian horses are traditionally favored in endurance racing and the tough Mongol horse is a far cry from their leaner, flashier cousins. And yet, these local horses naturally cover long distances as part of their normal days. More, they have incredible heart and take great care of their riders.

With four months of research prior to the event, and the travel debacles in air and on ground, the anticipation was electric. I had no experience, no ideas of the best angles to photograph the riders, but I had a lot of willingness to learn.

Dawn on the first day of the race was buzzing with excitement. The herdsmen had been up for hours collecting the horses as they had wandered off in the night. The riders were scattered trying to organize their gear, eat breakfast, and get used to the process.

Now in their second year, the event organizers were still fine-tuning the process. The idea was for the riders to deposit their saddles with each of their assigned rider numbers in the saddling area. They had the previous evening to sort their fenders, cage stirrups, and any seat savers they brought with them.

Soon, riders were trickling in with their equipment. The herders, under the guidance of Nara and Camille, were sorted into three categories of horses: heavyweight, those for the timid riders, and those remaining.

As horses were saddled by the nomads, some ridden for the rider, each would go through the initial vetting area to determine if they were sound.

Finally, after much excitement from, well everyone, they lined up at the starting line.

The special surprise? The Buddhist Lama was attending to bless the race, the riders, and the horses with a traditional blessing and offering.

The Buddhist Lama who blessed our event.

He was dressed in a glorious robe of yellow-gold like the sun, and with his blessing the riders began the race at a walk and then a gradual trot. I'd heard tales of other races, with a mad gallop out of the start gate, and the

Steward noted how sedately they began! Soon, however, many chose to canter, and very quickly small groups formed.

Immediately I became aware that this event was special. Rather than being timed, the race is points-based. The rules were created and adjusted to reflect the best of the Federation Equestrian Internationale (FEI), American Endurance Ride Conference (AERC), and the Australian Endurance Ride Association (AERA). With points there was less emphasis on speed and more on animal welfare and conditioning over the long distance, with special points awarded each day for the Best Condition and Best Sportsmanship recipients.

The first day took riders through grass, sand, standing water, a bridge, a village, and up and down hills. I chose to ride with Camille and get the lay of the land as I knew she would be everywhere, and I would have an idea where to take the best photographs.

Checkpoints were set on the course over the following distances: 15 kilometers, 30 km, 40, (mandatory 1-hour hold for lunch), 55 km, 70 km, and 80 km. Water, electrolytes, and some candies were provided at each checkpoint, along with a veterinarian inspection. It was fantastic for me to check in with the riders to hear their stories as they occurred and also learn who was perhaps having problems.

As we passed riders on the course, we found better action shots, but it was increasingly difficult to get good ones while moving over the rough terrain. By the end of the week I had learned that either using the GoPro, which had sponsored equipment for the event, or my phone worked better to get shots while moving. Alternatively, we would pull over and I would catch the riders coming by before hopping back into the lorry to beat the riders to their next checkpoint.

Every day was different. A different course and different terrain. Some courses were wide and flat, while others were more technical. The riders also rode with different people each day depending on their horses, some together in a pack and others just one or two.

The first day of the race was perhaps the hardest for most. The sun was brutal with little breeze to provide relief. Our Canadian rider wasn't drinking enough water and had to be forced to eat at the 40 kilometer checkpoint, but she chose to continue and did so under the guidance of an established endurance rider from Australia. His best friend, with whom he had traveled, felt guilty like she was pushing her horse too much. As a result, she chose to walk beside and astride for quite a distance, lagging behind under the watchful eye of the staff in case she decided to stop for the day.

That is the beautiful thing. Even though this is a race, at the end of the day it is ultimately an adventure. While vetting out or choosing to not complete the day resulted in zero points, riders are not pulled from the entire event. They continue the next day. No one is forced to ride or sent home packing.

But this rider did not choose to stop riding. Alone for almost half the ride, she continued on — upset, hot, tired, but determined to finish what she started.

Many of the riders chose to finish as a tie that first day.

As each rider finished, they asked about the others' welfare and commiserated over the day's events. Some went to relax after their horses were cared for or get some much-needed rest, but then one of the riders, Tania from Australia, came to ask if we could cheer the lagging rider on as she approached the finish. Some who knew this rider warned against it saying she would be embarrassed, but very quickly all the completed riders came together to support their companion and give her a pat on the back.

I learned a lot on this first day. I learned about long-distance riding, Mongolia, travel photography, but mostly, I learned about the incredible strength and heart of people.

As an introvert, I will often seek quiet and am quite happy being a hermit, venturing out only when I crave social interaction. I tend to choose animals over humans, but on the very first day, I saw the incredible heart of people and how they can come together to support each other.

Each day over the six days was a slightly different observation. Some riders progressed and seemed stronger over the ride, while others seemed to weaken and struggle mentally or physically.

———

DAY THREE I AWOKE TO THE SOUND OF RAIN POUNDING on the ger and rushed to make sure my equipment was dry. We dressed, breakfasted, and readied in the rain, but by the time the race began at 7 AM, over the horse line appeared a double rainbow. A sure sign of luck.

One of our Kiwi riders, Kaz, had a horse that was incredibly difficult to mount, and even reared for the herder holding him at a checkpoint. The sun came out to burn off the rain, and the riders stopped in a group to disrobe from their rain gear, leaving it in a pile on the ground which we picked up in the trucks.

From the very first moment we saw two riders really struggle to keep their horses moving. Separated from the group, the horses lost that herd-bound mentality that tends to keep them moving as a band. One of the riders decided he wasn't having fun and would never make the finish line in the allotted 12 hours, so he chose to bow out. He was picked up and his horse hobbled for a nomad to collect.

The other horse plodding along did meet with others and all three became quite slow. As we waited at the water trough checkpoint, we became concerned and had just decided to head back a bit when we saw four riders galloping toward us in the distance. Soon they arrived, three women and one of our herders who had collected the hobbled horse and was riding him back. He showed them how to move the horses and then encouraged them all to a race!

While well in the back of the pack, all three women had large smiles and an amazing story to bring home. More, one of our Mongolian veterinarians became envious and decided to ride out with them to the next checkpoint himself, mounting up and enjoying himself immensely.

———

SOME RIDERS TOOK THEIR ADVENTURES IN STRIDE AND kept their positivity while others had good and bad days. The race was simple, travel 480 kilometers over six days on six different horses, and yet each person had a different experience. It was truly amazing.

Each day I have a memory of the riders' adventures. I experienced it all from the ground, vicariously, and with mounting envy. Pun intended. While some of the horses were more sensitive, these people were challenging themselves and having the time of their lives experiencing Mongolia on horseback, the way it is meant to be appreciated.

I wasn't a rider; I was on the outside looking in. As such, I was tired but not sore, and brought home memories I will never forget. As an official, I had the luxury of seeing things behind the curtain and just how much work really goes into an event like this. It is actually astounding to be part of the effort of a 10-day event in an undeveloped country with people who do not speak the same language. I had the absolute pride in being even a small part of it all.

I would change nothing at all about my time with the race, and it gave me a new perspective. I didn't want to be just an observer. I, too, wanted to feel these horses under me and the wind in my hair with a Golden Eagle circling overhead.

12

WE'RE NOT IN JERSEY ANYMORE

Truthfully the basecamp, food, and toilets were much more than I had expected or envisioned, much to my relief. To my utter joy, I learned quickly that all the female officials, six of us, were to share a ger of our own. Living and working alongside these women you become close in a way only shared experience will do. Personal details like the number of siblings they have may yet to be learned, but I know that Ann, our FEI 3* Head Veterinarian, loves the color pink, brings a hair dryer in the hopes that she will get to use it even once during the journey, and that she hates mornings and needs eggs in her breakfast. We slept next to each other and ate together, often with her finishing the food I could never complete in one sitting. I would save her eggs so the riders didn't eat them all while she slowly woke. We joked that we were the married couple of the camp.

With my ger family member, Dr. Ann Lammens!

Camp became a source of comfort throughout the race. The race began each day at 7 AM and ended by 7 PM but, usually, the riders arrived by mid-afternoon. So we spent a good amount of time in our little village. While we moved camp every few days at least, sometimes once a day depending on the track, I would look for my ger and unload my bags.

Camp is easy to maneuver. Bright, generously sized blue tents for the riders on one side for their privacy.

A few green tents in the distance provided privacy for a a camp shower or two with a bucket outside for clothes washing, and two "toilets." Yes, holes dug in the ground, but provided was a toilet frame to sit on and toilet paper to absorb and drop in the hole. Not as basic as I had expected and pleasantly received.

At the center of it all is always a large, beautiful and open marquis for meetings and "family" meals. This was usually next to the coffee, tea, water tent and the catering tent where the magic happens. I am still amazed at the caterer and staff. How do you prepare food for 18 riders, seven officials, drivers and nomads with no electricity or refrigeration?

The marquis is the town hall, the center of the village. Riders usually need to decompress in their tents, and some like to party there for a while, but everything social occurs in the marquis. At any given time, you may find me on my computer downloading photos or jotting down notes for the day while someone has a much-needed cup of instant coffee and others chat with the veterinarians asking about the best way to take heart rate.

After dinner, those with energy remained to have a drink or two they may have bought at the local village grocery and play card games.

On day three, I remained behind after dinner with some riders instead of returning to the ger I shared with the officials. There was a small, beautiful pond in our view, near the horse line, and as the sun set, rider Stephanie braided my knotted hair, using a pen to separate the curls, (hey, camp showers and no conditioner), while we talked about home and horses. She and Kaz were best friends, closer than sisters, and I found myself laughing at their familiar nudges and sass to each other.

Later, with my hair in two beautiful braids so I wouldn't have to wash it again for a few days, I sat with Ruth and Mathilde who decided to play a game called Fluffy Bunny with marshmallows. I have no idea where those came from, but sweets had a way of showing up. Often, we'd stop at a local store to buy candy and sweets for the riders, and the riders also had the opportunity to buy whatever they wanted or needed from the small selections available. There I was laughing so hard I was crying, while Ruth and Mathilde stuffed their faces with these marshmallows and counting, "1 fluffy bunny, 2 fluffy bunny," trying to beat each other. I got it on video and had to post it to the event's Facebook page. After all, I wanted to show the fun that was being had!

Basecamp was a safe haven. Riders exhausted or exhilarated from the day would arrive, pass through vetting, or some eliminated, albeit very rare, and venture to their tents for some quiet, or to the marquis for some caffeine and social time. It was assumed, by me anyway, that if you were in the marquis you were willing to talk.

We didn't have a crazy tale to tell every night but when we did it was a great source of fun for us all to share in their experience.

————

PERHAPS MY FAVORITE BASECAMP PASTIME WAS THE story of the day. This "tradition" began on day three when we had three riders lose track of the course. They came back with the most amazing stories to share of their adventure, and so because they didn't finish we asked them to tell their tales to entertain everyone. The memory still makes me laugh.

I will try to tell the tale of Ruth and Tania, but I fear it will never be so good as the original. For that, you must visit the Gobi Desert Cup YouTube channel.

Here goes:

Tania and Ruth were acquaintances from home, trail riders and both moms wanting an adventure. They didn't always ride together during the race, it depended on their horses, but on this day their horses looked like twins and were brothers. They decided to stick together. Early on, they missed one of the pink ground markers at a turn and headed in the wrong direction unknowingly. After about five kilometers without seeing another marker, they knew they had gone the wrong way and turned back to retrace their steps.

They came up with the brilliant idea to draw an arrow with their initials in the sand track, indicating where they had gone once the officials realized they were off course. With checkpoints set up at 15 km, 30 km, 40 km, 55 km, 70 km, and 80 km for water and electrolytes for horses and riders, it was only a matter of time.

Unfortunately, Tania's horse was incredibly difficult to mount that day. She, with the tiniest bladder it became a running joke, decided to hold it for as long as possible. More, it meant poor Ruth had to keep mounting and dismounting to draw the signal while Tania looked on from astride.

After several signals, which they were smart enough to take photos of for their memories, Ruth went to remount. In her words, she "overshot the pony."

I can still remember the way she said it and want to collapse with laughter.

Mongolian horses have very sensitive right sides because they are never handled on that side, ever, and tacked up only on the left. They distrust anyone on their right side. She knew that. But she was used to larger horses and was getting tired. This time, she mounted as if her horse was larger and put too much of her body on the right side. As a result, he took off bucking.

In Ruth's words, "Buck, buck, B-U-C-K!"

And off she went, hitting the ground hard.

The trouble with small horses is that the ground is close so if you fall you don't have time to roll. You just splat.

Ruth lay there, her breath gone, while Tania sat still astride her horse determined to remain mounted and calling out, "Are you okay?"

Ruth got it all on her GoPro camera and later sent me the file, which I still watch when I'm in need of a good laugh. Don't get me wrong. It wasn't funny that she fell or had the wind knocked out of her. That would be mean. But the good spirits of these friends writing these signals and then, of course, Tania refusing to dismount but having to pee so badly, walking over to catch the loose horse for her friend. I know it's better in their words, but it still makes me laugh.

Afterward as Ruth remounted and they retraced their steps, they met a local nomad. He came down on horseback to greet the strangers and offered water for their horses. Then, using hand gestures he asked to race them and helped them back to the track. They had the adventure of their lives and a story that will never grow old.

This is the greatest gift of The Gobi Desert Cup. The opportunity for these women to come to Mongolia, and yes, race, but also to truly experience the culture. This story sticks in my brain because it is funny, but shows the openness, generosity, and fun of the local people. They truly enjoyed us visiting and would make efforts to come show off their wrestling skills or share a traditional blessing.

In New Jersey where I was raised, a stranger would be met with suspicion and a certain level of guardedness. That is not to say we are unfriendly, just untrusting. The local culture in Mongolia could not be more opposite.

Ruth and Tania had an interaction they will always remember, but so will this man. They did not speak the same language, and even using hand signals, there was some confusion. However, they will both remember this day for a long time.

They weren't the only ones with chance meetings brought by curiosity of the locals. Camille and I experienced two gentlemen on a motorcycle stopping by our checkpoint one day as we brought up the rear of the race. One nomad was dressed in a traditional deel with wide belt and Under Armour sneakers, of all things.

Nara, our friend was there and translated for us as these men presented us with a container of herbs to sniff in a traditional greeting. I was skeptical but unwilling to offend these nice men, and Nara assured us it was okay.

Boy was it pungent and burned the nose!

When I returned to camp, Nara's wife, Bara, asked about our visit and I told her of our interaction. She mimicked inhaling through the nose, and uttered "Ah, yes traditional greeting. Sniff, like cocaine."

The look on my face must have been priceless and full of horror because she started laughing uproariously. Okay, okay I can take a joke. I was nervous for a second there, but she was just teasing thankfully.

Every interaction was a positive one despite the serious lack of communication. As much as I tried to learn Mongolian, the language is incredibly hard to pronounce correctly. Our teenage interpreter wrote up a list of basic words, writing them out phonetically. I hope that will be a game changer!

13

FEAR OF MISSING OUT

I am lucky to be here. I am lucky to be here.

The refrain goes through my mind over and again. And I am. I feel it keenly. But, somehow, I went from being incredibly grateful to be an official documenting the event, to being slightly jealous of the riders.

Part of my job is to observe and to interview each rider about their experiences each day. With two days of basecamp and six full days of racing, I yearned to mount and ride a Mongolian horse. After all, I was in Mongolia, the horses were all around me, and the opportunity was so close I could literally touch it.

What surprised me was the lack of fear I felt. By nature, I'm a timid rider and don't take chances. Mongolian horses have a reputation as being semi-feral, and yet, during my week I noticed how calm, docile, and, dare I say, forgiving they were to the western riders. The logical part of my brain knew they had received special conditioning and training for the event. More, the same horses participate each year. Another part of me wondered if it was because of the incredible horsemanship I saw by the riders.

Of course, there were blips. A horse that caused a little trouble and had to be ridden by a nomad, or another that was too sensitive on the right side, or what I liked to call the "no-no" zone.

These horses had earned my respect, and I thought to myself, "I'm here, I have to try." There was talk throughout the event, whispers that there may be an official's race. The term "race" had me nervous, as speed and competition are not my comfort zone. Still, the opportunity to ride was something that I couldn't, wouldn't resist.

I was excited!

And then the Gobi Desert Cup ended. The last riders came across the finish line, exhausted and proud. Some of the riders who had already passed the vet check, lay napping in the sand dunes, recharging. We were spent. Very quickly, the herders loaded the horses to be driven back to their homes. Part of me was relieved that the decision to ride was taken from me, but the other part was disappointed.

Very quickly, I learned they held a few horses for the seven of us officials to race, one kilometer across the steppe from the finish line to the horse line at basecamp. The rules? Cross first. The 18 riders lost no time taking bets on the winner. Two very kindly told me they bet on me. The last thing I needed was pressure, and I knew that given the opportunity I'd probably back off, slow down, and walk across the finish line just proud that I finished, even in last place.

With the powerful mixture of anticipation, nerves, and mounting trepidation, I prepared to ride. My tension was palpable, and my face must have been ghostly white because Bara, who is in charge of camp, asked me if I was okay. I could only nod and tell her honestly, "I want a very safe horse, like one you would put a child on."

Of course, I laugh now because, hello! Jockeys in Mongolia are all children as they are lighter and faster on horseback. Still, somehow, they knew what I meant, and our herder gave me one of his horses who he promised is "kind and gentle." So I mounted up.

Me and "Spanky" before the race.

I was shaking, literally shaking. I'm a timid rider. I'm *The Timid Rider*, for goodness sake. And for very good reason. I was completely outside of my comfort zone. This was taking bold to a whole new level, and I kept asking myself if this was worth it. What if I got hurt in Mongolia? It's an undeveloped country and the closest hospital was 800 kilometers away at least.

Everyone rallied around me, the nomads, the officials, and the riders alike. When we realized one saddle was missing, I volunteered to get off and just not ride. Of course, Camille wouldn't hear of it. She knew if I got off, I wouldn't get back on. After working together for four months and living together for two weeks, she had a handle on my moods.

But the fear of missing out kept me in that saddle. When would I have another chance to ride a Mongolian horse? I would never forgive myself. With the encouragement of my friends and new family, I mustered the courage to sit on top of that pony. More, I started talking to him.

True connection is voiceless, wordless. I'd seen firsthand how quickly these horses would respond to connection. As they are semi-feral their very lives depend on it after all. But I lacked trust in myself and shamefully in my horse. So, I did what makes me comfortable and started to communicate with him vocally. I nicknamed him "Spanky" because he looked like a kid's pony I knew from my home barn. More, he felt like a Spanky. The Mongolians do not name their horses but generally call them by a description like "fast" or "brown with white spot."

Once all the other officials were mounted and we were moving, the anticipation was over. For me, the waiting is the hardest part. When we were moving it became official and there was no turning back. I took up the rear walking to the start line, getting to know how my horse responded. He was actually quite slow and would linger in the back, so I gave the nomadic signal to move, "Choo-choo" and off we would trot until we reached the others.

I was told throughout the race that the horses had choppy strides because of their conformation. However, I am quite used to riding small horses and ponies, and also quite short myself, so I wasn't remotely uncomfortable. Of course, I was only trotting a short distance as opposed to 80 kilometers like the riders did each day, so it wasn't exactly a fair comparison.

Camille kept turning around to check on me, and I think she finally realized how nervous I was. What she didn't tell me until later was that it was the first time she'd ridden since she became pregnant.

As we neared the start, she took pity and announced,

"We'll start with a walk, then a trot, then canter, and not gallop until the end." I nodded in agreement and with relief.

Turning my horse, Camille and I were in front. She began to trot, and my horse broke into a nice, collected canter. Well, to an FEI 3* rider that is quite the challenge. She shouted, "So it's like that," and took off into a ground-eating gallop.

Well, crap.

Crap, crap, crap.

Sometimes you have to know when to hold on and then there are others when you must let go. I chose the latter. Why fight it? So there we were, galloping neck and neck, Camille on the track with a huge grin on her face and me off to her side on the grass. I looked for marmot holes and asked her to move over, where she replied sassily, "No, it's a race!"

My usually non-existent competitive streak kicked in. I shocked even myself that we were tied for more than half the race, so I just held on to the front of the Franco-C Renegade saddle and focused on breathing. I had to trust my horse.

It seemed a long distance because of the fear, and I'm unused to riding longer distances at fast paces. Suburban New Jersey doesn't have many gallops after all. The next thing I knew my assistant photographer and course veterinarian, Dr. Julie Kemp, came flying up on my right her arms and legs wildly flapping in the air like she was running barrels. Soon after, FEI 4* veterinarian Dr. Ian Baines came on the left, his legs so long they almost reached the ground.

Alas I came across finish line in 4th place, behind admittedly accomplished riders, to the cheers and catcalls of riders and nomads alike. I'll never forget the feeling of accomplishment I felt. I did it!

Words cannot express that moment. Our audience was a blur, the noise in the background, but I remember unclenching one white-knuckled first from the saddle to give a thumbs up as I passed by with a smile. My horse slowed to a canter just before the finish and was easily brought back. I hopped off to back pats and accolades. No, I didn't come in first place. But I did win.

I rode that Mongolian horse at a full gallop in the Gobi Desert and did it well. I was proud of myself. Nothing felt like victory more.

Soon after, Nara and Ann arrived at a trot, Ann shouting, "I got the donkey!" We all found it incredibly hilarious because it was so obvious she was frustrated but laughing it off. Her horse just didn't have that go button and Nara, ever the gentlemen, stayed behind in his traditional wooden saddle to ride with her.

We were all in amazing spirits and ready to celebrate the end of the race! The Gobi Desert Cup tests us all mentally and physically whatever your role in the event. Finally, I was a rider, even for a short distance, and didn't miss out on anything. The experience is something of which I'm incredibly proud and hope to do again. But that first time will never be topped. I didn't let my nerves stop me. I truly felt like this timid rider conquered something that day.

14

HUMP DAY

A s a special surprise, Camille and Bara had organized a fun day for the riders to celebrate the end of our adventure. Everyone was exhausted but looking forward to more cultural experiences.

Our first stop took us off the highway and onto, well, nothing. There were no tracks to follow, no basic dirt roads. Only a few of us, the 18 riders, seven officials, and our drivers with Bara and our interpreters were in attendance.

There was a small lot to park with vendors, and when we arrived, we learned that we were at Black Mountain, one of the seven sacred Khan Mountains. Each mountain is occupied by a ghost, (or spirit), and this particular one was male. As such, only men were allowed to the very top.

Many women were annoyed but while disappointed in theory, (I really didn't want to walk all the way up because I'm lazy), I understood this is a cultural difference. After all, there were other sacred mountains dedicated to women.

We toured, climbing past a large Buddha on a pedestal and walking along pathways framed with colorful flags. There was a serenity to the mountain, a stillness, and I felt grateful to be there. During the race we were running from checkpoint to checkpoint working our tails off. Here at the mountain, I was exhausted but I felt happy to be experiencing the culture with nothing else to focus on.

The goats were my favorite. These goats frolicked and ran around following visitors, usually in a cluster, although at one point I spied a goat with large horns climbing the Buddha. It amazes me how nimble they are on the rocky soil and steep grades. My friend Ann and I found each other and played a bit with these goats, kneeling to take photos. Daring? Perhaps, but they were friendly and spent a little time chewing my bracelets, making me laugh. For a time, they followed behind, likely hopeful for food but sadly disappointed.

We had only a short time on the mountain because we

were running late, a chronic problem in Mongolia as time tends to follow strange guidelines, and we all met at the vendors' area below. This was my first view of artisan-crafted materials because I never had time to visit the Black Market with the others before the race since my plane was, ahem, delayed.

Some of the crafts were obviously manufactured but still beautiful. With the help of our lovely young interpreter, I purchased a prayer bowl for my mother, who is a shaman, and a small, beaded bracelet to add to my collection. I buy a new one in each country I travel. It is distinct and every time I wear it, I remember this moment and my time in Mongolia.

When we got back into the trucks, I sat behind the driver facing the rear.

Sadly, that was not a smart idea.

I've never been carsick in my life.

We were going somewhere, even I didn't know, and directly over the desert. The windows were cracked but it was hot in the truck. The heat, the bouncing, and the rear view created a problem with nausea.

The ground was a formidable opponent. The dips, the bouncing, and the swerving did nothing for my stomach as I gritted my teeth and told myself I had to make it work. Once, we passed another of our lorries which had stopped to let out one of the riders to vomit on the ground. He'd ridden 480 kilometers for the last six days, but this truck ride across the desert was what did him in.

We stopped again a while later for another vomit session, poor guy, and many other riders took the opportunity to relieve themselves. I looked out the window to see four or five of the females lined up facing the trucks to all urinate. Gone was the attempt to walk off into the distance. We were officially indoctrinated.

I still have no idea how long it took to arrive at our destination, perhaps several hours. I'm not convinced the drivers weren't lost. (We found our way back to the highway later much more quickly.) But soon, we arrived to our special surprise. Bactrian camels!

We had seen these unique camelids from afar, wandering with their herds. But nothing prepared us for the smell up close; they were nose-piercingly pungent.

I jumped off the bus, almost pushing people out of the way, and gulped fresh air. The entire trip I had maintained calm and a modicum of professionalism. But here I was, on the last day, kneeling on the ground trying not to vomit as my stomach bounced around against my other internal organs. It took a good 15 minutes or so, but finally I recovered and was able to enjoy the spectacle in front of me. I was grateful it didn't take longer because it was probably dangerous to be kneeling as I was on the ground next to these huge camels. Their feet were bigger than my head!

As a child I'd ridden a camel at the Bronx Zoo, back when they did that sort of thing. A Bactrian camel exists only in Mongolia and is quite unique. They were larger than I remembered, and I laughed as I watched the riders mount with the help of the camel jockeys and try to figure out how to steer. The camel jockeys use one rein attached to a needle in the nostril of the animal. We were definitely not in our comfort zone as horse riders. I volunteered to go in the second group, content to let someone else figure it out first.

The first wave of riders would be racing, but also were tasked with riding their animals to the start point through the canyon. The scent of musk was thick and many of the men loudly complained about their nether regions being squished. Alas, sometimes it is truly a good thing to be a girl.

If you have never seen a camel race or ridden one for yourself, I highly recommend it. Camels by nature are quite docile and it is virtually impossible to fall off — especially with two humps to nestle between! As the first race ended, the riders were full of excitement and adrenaline; they came back and at least three recommended their quiet ones for me to ride, knowing me well as they now did.

When the camel kneeled down to accept me, I remember thinking to myself, "How I am possibly going to get my leg over?" I'm only five feet tall, and this camel, even kneeling, was still taller than me. The camel jockey helped steady me as I very ungracefully managed to raise my leg high enough to hover it between humps. The stirrups were luckily very short already, and I was good to go!

I had a short panic attack, kept carefully to myself, when my camel first rose. They rock forward and backward to free their legs. Once aloft, all the camels herded together. You can try to move them but soon you just go with it and avoid your friends' feet.

Finally, an animal that is virtually impossible to fall from.

SOON, WE WERE OFF A SHORT DISTANCE TO THE START point. Camels are so slow! Looking out into the horizon, astride this rare camel, I thought of how far I'd come in my own journey. Only a few months ago I was mourning the loss of my massage business, but I began to open myself up to new opportunities and truly tested myself time and again. I passed these tests and came out the stronger for it.

Nothing gave me more pride than racing that horse across a short expanse of desert, and now here I was just 24 hours later determined to do the same on a camel. The horse race had a bit of foreshadowing because once again I found myself neck and very long camel neck at the front with Camille Champagne. She has a competitive drive like I've never seen! She saw me and was off like a shot in the ground eating, side-to-side amble that camelids have with me directly to the side just behind her.

Off to my side I spied Dr. Baines trying to usurp my position once again and gave a firm "Choo-choo!" to my mount, urging him forward with a huge smile on my face. I was laughing, the wind in my hair, and came in 2nd place to the applause of my friends. Who knew I could ride a camel better than a horse and with more confidence?

I'll never forget that moment. I let my anxiety go and for a brief moment felt what others likely do: freedom and excitement. It was glorious.

15

CELEBRATION

The final days of the race were hot and filled with stories and adventures. The final vet check was longer than normal and instead of having some time to relax, the riders were entertained by the officials' race. By the end of the week everyone was exhausted. Very tired men and women celebrated with warm liquor and a surprise karaoke machine mean trouble follows closely behind.

Everyone was ready to let loose. I won't divulge secrets. After all, what happens in the desert stays in the desert, and comparatively to the modern Western world, the transgressions were minor and few. Food was buffet style, dancing was prevalent, especially with our rider Howard who was quite skilled in ballroom, and everyone was looking to relax after the race completed.

Some perhaps drank too much but I make no judgment.
Who hasn't been there?

Officials with one of our riders, Howard!

*Getting to know each other at basecamp after the
Opening Ceremony.*

What I found most poignant was the camaraderie. We, virtual strangers, traveled to this remote country where English is hardly spoken. Officials, riders, and nomads all converging for this one pocket in time. We laughed together, bathed pretty much together because camp showers are a little awkward, slept together in tents or gers. We were a village, a community. Dare I say, it felt like a family.

Like most families, we don't always get along. There is a natural and needed divide between the officials and the riders. Officials must observe the rules of the race and treat everyone fairly. I alone had some leeway because it was my job to share their experience with their families at home. As such, I built relationships with the riders, some close and others not so much. Yet the other officials were set apart. We were all polite, of course, but aware of the jobs we had to do.

After the final race, we were all happy to celebrate together and let loose, officials and riders alike. We needed it.

Some celebrated the end of their journey while others acknowledged their success for meeting their personal goals. There were no winners and no losers as the race results would not be announced until the closing ceremony.

For the first time all week, we were all determined to appreciate the unique opportunity we experienced together. There were highs and lows for everyone. Some missed their families immensely and were unable to contact them; others had equipment delayed at the start having been lost by the airline. Then there were those who pushed themselves too hard so they were unable to ride the next day, forced to take a break because the desert is unforgiving.

Some of us dealt with family and personal issues with others at camp. One even found out she was pregnant, something she had not planned but was cautiously optimistic.

We had inside jokes and indelible memories. No one was left untouched.

For me, I had accomplished something that I never anticipated. No, correction, I accomplished many things, and I surprised even myself. That night I celebrated taking the chance to apply for The Gobi Desert Cup, traveling to Asia, being an official in an endurance race, trying and failing to learn Mongolian, and racing a native horse across the steppe like Genghis Khan in the 13th century. This unlikely adventurer and timid rider proved to herself that she *can* and she *will*. I am more than I thought. I am bold, and I am moving forward. I can acknowledge my nerves and try to overcome them, opening the road to bigger and better things.

There is nothing so bonding as living in the wild together for ten days, brought together by mutual passion and experience. I spoke with the riders well in advance of the ride, helping them to prepare and learning their stories. As a result, I felt like I knew them. This only grew while I interviewed each about their experiences in and out of the saddle, danced with them in the marquis, or drank together over a game of cards or a silly game of Fluffy Bunny. Our time together at meals, checkpoints, and at basecamp created a small village in a way. There were no secrets. We, together, experienced the adventure of a lifetime that most will never have the opportunity to see.

16

COMING BACK DOWN

Saying goodbye to the riders was hard. I would travel back with Lorie, Allan, and Bob on the first leg of the journey to Beijing. All of us adventurers become close after spending ten days in our own small village. But when it came time to say goodbye to Camille, Ann, Ian, Rosie, and the other officials, I cried. In the middle of the hotel lobby, surrounded by friends, I grieved the loss of people who had become so special to me in so short a time.

I knew that my life had changed forever. I hoped to become a permanent part of this amazing event and had a list of reasons why I wanted to return. But the biggest was so that I could spend time with these amazing people: the officials who leave their everyday lives to run this race, the veterinarians who selflessly care for these animals, and the nomads who work 20 hours per day to make sure our riders have the experience of their lives. The local Mongolians embrace the event and celebrate it.

While I was still "plugged" into the world, posting updates about the event on Facebook whenever possible, my time in the vast countryside caused me to reset myself. I felt a change in priority and a feeling that may only be explained as a grounding.

So often we race from one moment to the next, our heads dipped and attention on our screens. I confess I do the same. But feeling the earth beneath my body, resting at a checkpoint while my hair blew in the breeze and Golden Eagles circled above, and camels grazed several kilometers into the horizon — this land gave me back something I didn't know that I was missing.

I traveled back home, exhausted but happy and so excited to see my family again. I found the best version of myself once again, the elusive happy and independent Heather. The woman who existed not as a wife or mother, but somehow more than either and also *less*, more basic.

Upon my return to Beijing Airport I was prepared. By this time, I knew the airport like the back of my hand and luckily had checked most of my bags through to home. I had only my camera equipment, so surely this would be a cake walk.

Of course not! Did you not read my previous experience in Beijing?

I traveled from UB to Beijing with three riders, two of whom had a flight leaving 40 minutes before us. We disembarked the plane and walked with purpose through the international arrivals, passport checks, and then:

Bam!

Security was incredibly backed up. So, I did what any obnoxious traveler would do, I pushed through the line telling them my flight was leaving (true) and bringing my three friends with me. Security was thorough once again, but thankfully I had to go through only once this time around. Once through, no one had waited for me, even the rider on my own flight, and with the forethought to ask the information desk my gate, ran full out directly there.

I am so not a runner.

I arrived, sweating and smelling, but last in line to the boarding gate, breathing a sigh of relief. My flight wasn't supposed to depart for an hour, but I knew Beijing. Let this be a lesson for you all traveling to and from Mongolia and Beijing airport…have a layover of at least four hours and camp out at the gate. Do not leave. Thankfully, I made it and the travel home was perfect.

However, I didn't realize how hard it would be to be this Mongolian version of myself at home.

My flight landed on time, but the bags never arrived. I sat at the carousel for hours looking for them, when, finally, I found out they never left Ulaanbataar. Leaving the baggage area, I was met with a banner and three screaming daughters, excited for my return!

I was home.

The most beautiful of all views.

I sometimes complain about my children, how they

don't listen, or they cause stress. But they are mine, and I love them immensely. It took my traveling to the other side of the world to realize just how much of my world revolves around them. I want to be a good example for them and someone they can look up to and depend on.

My husband had a less effusive greeting due to having to deal with our dogs attacking a groundhog and killing it moments before leaving for the airport. I didn't realize what he had experienced, but I was disappointed he didn't seem happier to see me. I was so excited to be back and talk to them about my time away. But I was so in my own world that I never took a second to realize how hard it must have been for them to be home and unable to talk to me often. My husband had work and the children. I had fun and adventure.

For two weeks I was completely independent, but I had left a family behind. While I missed them, they had their own experiences both good and bad. I think we all learned a little something during my extended time in Asia. It took a month or two for me to reacclimatize to life as a working mom. I struggled to catch up with work, follow up on Gobi Desert Cup post-event deadlines, and also make up for time missed as a wife and mother.

It's a delicate balance, and one that I haven't perfected. But I'm working on it.

17

CAMILLE CHAMPAGNE

You have to know that you make a difference. When I began writing about my life and experiences it was very cathartic. I never realized the anxiety I held within until I began to spew words of honesty on paper and on the blog. The relief I felt afterward was incredible because getting my thoughts out provided a certain clarity. The next step was sharing these thoughts. That first time I hit "publish," it was terrifying, and yet the comments started flooding in. People I knew would stop me and say how they read my words and then they'd *thank me* for being so honest. I'm not sure I expected that. But more, people who didn't know anything about horses read to support me and related to my story because they have felt similar feelings in other areas of their lives.

I stopped writing just for myself. I confess that I still write for me because it makes me feel good and helps to process my feelings. However, I'm inspired by those people who do not feel comfortable voicing their feelings of uncertainty, doubt, and, yes, fear in their lives. So, I increasingly write to motivate and inspire those readers no matter their experience with horses.

I have much to learn about myself, my writing, and the world. Inevitably there will be trolls and haters who want to tear me down because I am trying to lift others up. I don't focus on those people; I feel sorry for them. Instead I focus on the people in my life who have similar goals and passions — for example, those people who want to lift others up.

Ride Founder and Director, Camille Champagne
with one of her "brother" nomads.

I'm lucky to have a few of those people in my life. One is Camille Champagne. Things in life happen for a reason. When you are on the correct path it seems that things just fall into place so easily. The Gobi Desert Cup and Camille are each one of those things.

You've now heard my introduction on how I became involved with this endurance race and what I experienced. Camille interviewed me via Skype, and we talked on the phone at least once per week for hours about the event, her plans, my ideas, and touching briefly on personal things.

However, arriving in Mongolia the first time and

meeting her in person was odd. We'd connected by
phone and social media often and to meet IRL (in real
life) was surreal. But Mongolia in itself is
unpredictable, and we had so much work to do in two
short weeks that we had to jump right into business.
And that's exactly what we did after my two-day travel
experience through the wilds of Beijing International
Airport and into dusty Ulaanbataar.

In many ways I identified with the riders. They could
never be truly prepared for the experiences of Mongolia
and The Gobi Desert Cup, and I myself was in the same
position. We were all first-timers, wide-eyed and taking
everything in. Yet, I was technically an official, and as
such, it was assumed I knew more than the riders.

Camille and I hit the ground running, as did the rest of
the officials. I was learning on the fly about Mongolia
and how best to do my job without prior experience in a
third-world country in, dare I say, rustic conditions?

Camille astounded me. I knew she had passion, but her
drive and dedication blew me away. Shortly after I was
hired, she let loose a little secret that she was pregnant.
The big part was that she was due just before the race! I
still don't know how she focused on her health, moving
to a new home, preparing for her baby, and planning the
second Gobi Desert Cup. She is truly an inspiration.

She is a very private person and quite shy, so to share

this with me and the beautiful photo of her and baby Charlotte in the hospital three weeks before the event meant a lot to me. In person, Camille is very serious while working. She expects the best out of everyone because she expects the best of herself. But this isn't an unreasonable expectation; in fact, she will do everything in her power to help that person to be their best. And that is what makes Camille that much more special. I wanted her to be happy with choosing me to work with her event.

Camille would wake at 4 AM every morning while the herders began to venture out onto the steppe to round up the roaming horses. Privately, as we would pass through a тосгон/"town," she would gather ingredients for breakfast that she would make for her Mongolian brothers in their camp. I am not sure the riders ever realized she did this. Camille was everywhere behind the scenes and overseeing everything to guarantee the herders, horses, officials, and riders all had an amazing experience. As a result, the other officials had more face time with the riders.

That second Gobi Desert Cup race was truly hard for Camille. She had to leave her newborn baby behind at home, still healing from the labor and complications she experienced. She was hormonal, emotional, and missing her child. Keeping busy helped but as she often says, "Mongolia will test you." Camille was tested as well and came out stronger because of it. But she didn't have to do it alone because she had our support. I must say, she held it together very well and was professional throughout. Most people had no idea what she was experiencing personally.

Support is the bottom line. The event wasn't perfect and there were certainly people, and occurrences, that created difficulty throughout that we had to manage and adjust expectations. After all, this is Mongolia. But neither the riders nor the officials were ever alone.

I observed this early on, and I think this is a big part of why the event means so much to me. An endurance race across the Gobi Desert has a way of revealing the best and worst of ourselves. Time and again I watched as riders, herdsmen, and officials cheered others on or offered words of encouragement to those who were struggling. Of course, there weren't all highs. Many experienced moments of frustration, trepidation, exhaustion, and more. But these were minor compared to the larger feeling of accomplishment.

Without technology and living together with only basic amenities, we become a small village dependent on each other for survival. This wasn't *Lord of the Flies*, survival of the fittest. This was *Utopia*.

I took this message home with me, understanding much more about what it means to stop focusing on yourself and how to support others. Motherhood is an amazing daily reminder as well, let me tell you.

I didn't realize that I was a source of support for Camille at the time. It was many months later when Camille wrote a short piece on me for the Gobi Desert Cup blog that I understood I did more than help her with the social media and marketing for her event. Sure, she told me repeatedly that I was doing a good job and always thanked me for my work, making me feel appreciated.

Used to internalizing my feelings, I cried at the words she wrote, which I since included in the foreword with her permission. These were a surprising gift in a world where strangers hide behind words to tear each other down. More, as a mother and wife, I often feel under appreciated or lacking, never being quite enough.

We may live across the world, and we may be a decade in age apart, (I'm older), but I found in Camille someone who has my back just as I have hers. It is an incredibly priceless gift.

We planned to attend the American Endurance Ride Conference (AERC) in Reno, Nevada, in March of 2019. Our 2018 winning Team USA would be in attendance and it would be Camille's first time in the United States. As such she wanted to make the most of it and visit our training partner, Christoph Schork's

Global Endurance Training Center in Moab, Utah. The next thing I know, I'm being invited to do some photographing and filming there, when she so casually mentions that I should ride 30 kilometers with them.

Hahahaha!

I laughed out loud until I realized she was serious. She is sneaky like that. "Oh Heather, you always impress me. You are the Timid Rider, and yet you challenge yourself." See? It's diabolical. But it works! Because then I start thinking how I would love to ride one of Christoph's horses and learn from him. How honored I would be to ride with both him and Camille who have thousands of miles under their belts in multiple countries.

Then, I think about how I am less than fit and unable to ride the distances they are accustomed. I would hold them back. I'm disappointed at my own thoughts because this is several months in the future and I should start exercising and take the opportunity handed to me on a silver platter. I say that I'll think of about it, which I do all night long. The possibility of letting them down is daunting and nerve-wracking. I naturally assumed I would disappoint while Camille had faith I would rise to the challenge.

In truth, Camille was shocked I didn't tell her to back off, and being the ambitious woman she is, decided to up the ante. Not one day later, we are talking on the phone about a new rider for the next year's GDC when she drops another bombshell on me.

You ready? I wasn't.

The words that came out of her mouth were so farfetched that I really didn't believe it. "I think you should race in The Gobi Desert Cup."

I couldn't even laugh. For once in my life, I was speechless. I mean, what?

It's one thing to try and ride in Utah at a training center for fun, which I had not yet agreed to do, by the way. It's an entirely different beast to consider spending a few years training to ride 300 miles across the Gobi Desert six days in a row on six different Mongolian horses.

And yet, I didn't immediately say no.

Sadly, while I had begun to get excited to ride with Christoph in Utah, my schedule prevented it and Camille rode there without me. But my disappointment eased when she traveled to New Jersey with her beautiful baby to visit me afterward, and we were able to spend a few days together as friends, touring my favorite places, including my barn, meeting my pony, and shopping in New York City. We made our own memories there apart from the race. We had lived together in Mongolia and it was wonderful and strange for her to see me at home, in such a different setting. In many ways it brought us closer together.

I will honestly consider riding in The Gobi Desert Cup one day. I didn't tell her to back off or laugh in her face for my own lack of faith in my abilities, although they were there. I kept thinking back to how I watched in envy as the riders cantered across the steppe, sometimes together, sometimes alone, but always making incredible memories. I thought of how I mounted "Spanky," the bay Mongolian horse I rode in the officials' race that the last day, galloping one kilometer to the finish line to the cheers of our riders. The feeling of adrenaline and accomplishment because I did something that challenged me, and I loved it.

So, with a big gulp, I penciled myself in for a future race. My husband came home to find me shell-shocked, and I expected him to finally put his foot down and tell me "no," but he didn't. He supported me and told me I should do it, and, honestly, I find myself humbled by the support.

As a mother, I often place others' needs ahead of my own. This also carries forward to my clients when I book a massage appointment on days that I usually reserve for errands or other important things. I do it because they need me. I do not often think about what I need. So for me to have the support of friends and family is priceless.

I hit the jackpot when I joined The Gobi Desert Cup because it made me a better version of myself and gave me friends who have become family. We may not agree on everything, but they always have my back when it counts, and they believe in me more than I believe in myself.

Now, I probably won't sleep well until I race the event myself. Having the support and belief of someone so incredibly hard-working and loyal as Camille creates a foundation on which you can believe in yourself. The journey isn't over. It is just the beginning.

18

TIMID IS NOT A FOUR-LETTER WORD

"Timid" is not a four-letter word. For all you smart asses out there, yes it has five letters. You know what I mean. It is not something to be ashamed of, a curse, or a dirty secret to hide away in a dark corner. I don't care what your passion is, your work, or your inspiration. All of us have occasional self-doubt or moments where we lack confidence.

I call myself "The Timid Rider" because I sometimes lack confidence in my riding ability, and I'm incredibly careful, but I'm not afraid of horses. Obviously, I am not afraid to challenge myself. I do, from time to time, doubt that I am any good. I question my equitation. I question my writing ability. I question my successes as a mother and wife.

The point is not to celebrate these feelings; in fact, it is quite the opposite. I want to acknowledge the emotions that are holding me back, and in doing so, keep moving forward. As my new friend Camille quotes from Lao Tzu, "The journey of a thousand miles begins with one step." The first step is admitting that I am not perfect.

With all the bragging and showing only the positive on social media by pretty much everyone, we are inundated with these high expectations and visuals of people living their lives to the fullest. But it isn't realistic. While I choose to focus on the positive because I'm annoyingly perky, I acknowledge that there are things I would improve about myself.

I began my blog, *The Timid Rider*, as a release for my own feelings. It made me more self-aware. But very quickly after seeing the engagement from others who could relate to me, I realized that I'm not just writing for myself. I am sharing my story with the intention of starting the conversation and letting others know that it is okay to feel you aren't good enough and you aren't alone.

Funny how I started my life as an introvert and yet ended up wanting to increasingly feel a sense of community. This world does not embrace those with inverted tendencies, for good or ill, and so I rose to the challenge and taught myself to be more comfortable, albeit awkward socially and in large gatherings.

Life is about adapting and changing when necessary. I've learned the most over the years by doing things that make me nervous. It isn't always pretty, and it doesn't always work out the way I intend, but I wouldn't have half the successes or fond memories I do now if I didn't at least try.

I hope that knowing this about me will be explain how a self-proclaimed "timid rider" would even think about venturing to Mongolia with people she had never met, alone and far from her friends and family, for an event she wouldn't dare dream to participate in herself.

This is that story, and I hope you enjoyed it. More than anything, I hope it inspires you to do something that challenges you, and in doing so prove that you are so much stronger and braver than you knew. You never know, perhaps we will one day meet on your own adventure in Mongolia should you choose to race.

So, my friend, I am giving myself a new goal. While I'm officially the Media Coordinator, I've decided that I need to experience all sides. I plan to train and prepare to ride in The Gobi Desert Cup myself, officially. I am committing to the training and preparation involved, and as a Type A, it may take a little time, possibly years. While it is fun being an official, I need to see how the other side lives! I'm nervous but excited. I want to challenge myself again in a new way.

#BeBold

THE TIMID RIDER

I will need to get in better physical shape, learn endurance techniques and rules, and ride more than five miles in distance at a time. More, I'll need to mentally push myself because it would be so easy to say, "I can't do this." The truth is, I know that I can, and I want to try. I'm hoping I can get a few other timid riders to join me on my journey so we can do it together. I don't need to win, but I do want to finish. And that, will be the best feeling of accomplishment in the world.

ACKNOWLEDGEMENTS

Thank you for picking up my book. Even more, thank you for finishing it!

My entire life I've loved two things: writing and animals. Because I was afraid of not living up to my own expectations, I stepped away from my dreams for too many years. This is the story of how I again found my passion, and what I've experienced as a result. I am still a work in progress.

Sometimes taking the long way around teaches you more about yourself than you could have dreamed. I believe that every decision I made led me to this point and gave me an experience, or expertise, that I would need to succeed at what I love.

A lot of work goes into realizing a dream. I wouldn't be

here without the support of my husband and our daughters. Their support and belief in me means the world.

Why should you read my story? Because I am you. Whether you are an equestrian, a mom, a dad, a pet parent, or someone else entirely, each of you have something about which you are passionate. Perhaps in the normal day-to-day grind you've forgotten what excites you, or pushed it aside for a while. Perhaps you are just too afraid to fail. I've lived my life going above and beyond to do everything except what really matters to me. My own dream.

I'm not afraid to fail anymore because my passion is greater than my fear. You are reading my personal journey.

If my story inspires you, or just plain entertains you, please take a few minutes and leave a review and tell your friends. As an independent author I do it all on my own and reviews mean so much.

If you are interested in my future books, please follow me on Facebook, Twitter, or on Amazon and Goodreads. Don't forget to follow my adventures on my blog, *The Timid Rider*!

ALSO BY HEATHER WALLACE

Books

Confessions of a Timid Rider

Equestrian Handbook of Excuses

The Equestrian Handbook of Excuses (Photography Edition)

Blog

The Timid Rider

Podcast

Equestrian Pulse Podcast

ABOUT THE AUTHOR

Heather Wallace is a Certified Equine Sports Massage Therapist (ESMT), Certified Canine Massage Therapist (CCMT), and Aromatherapist based in Monmouth County, New Jersey. Her fulfilling day job and a very understanding husband help her to pay the bills so she can accomplish her dream of being an author and travel the world.

Heather has written for a number of publications including *Equine Info Exchange*, *Sidelines Magazine*, and *Holistic Horse Magazine,* but her real love is her blog, *The Timid Rider*.

Her first book, *Equestrian Handbook of Excuses*, was a 2017 Literary Selection for the Equus Film Festival and is a humorous look at the excuses we tell ourselves on why we can't ride that day. Her second book, *Confessions of a Timid Rider*, details her insights about being an anxiety-ridden but passionate equestrian and writer. It was both an Amazon #1 Hot New Release and won the Equus Film Festival Winnie Award for Non-Fiction.

In her spare time, of which she has little, she spends her time with her husband, three children, two dogs, and pony.

Heather wears many hats and is extremely proud to be an example to her three daughters of a woman who follows her passion and faces challenges head on. Heather is every woman who decided to leave her fears behind to do what she loves.

Follow her on social media @timidrider or at timidrider.com.

facebook.com/timidrider

twitter.com/timidrider

instagram.com/timidrider

EXCERPT FROM CONFESSIONS OF A TIMID RIDER

The Grey Pony Incident

My first time independently on a horse was…interesting.

I was what you would call a horse-obsessed child. Shocking, I know. Instead of imaginary friends, I had an imaginary barn full of horses in my backyard. I dreamed of owning a barn one day and breeding Arabians, because they were the most beautiful horses I could dream of at the time. I had stuffed horses, Breyer horses, and read as many fiction and non-fiction horse books as I could get my hands on. Obsessed? Perhaps, but I prefer extremely passionate.

There is something inherently noble and graceful about horses. The fact that they trust humans, and allow us to share their lives, is a never-ending blessing for me. We all have something we feel connected to, and for me it has always been horses.

I begged to do pony rides at every local circus, party, or event I attended as a child. My parents would shake their heads and laugh, but it was so exciting!

However, my first independent experience on horseback didn't go the way I'd dreamed and planned. In fact, it didn't really go at all.

Family vacations should be filled with wonderful memories, and they usually are quite unforgettable. The petty family squabbles or sisterly bickering take a back seat to the new and amazing experiences, and you mostly remember the good times. A trick of our brains that make us do it again and again.

So goes our family trip to Arizona when I was about nine years old. I can still see the dust kicking up as our rental car pulled into the stable yard. My young brain did not take into account the details of the landscape, or the wooden sign marked "Trail Rides." Oh no, the anticipation of riding a horse in the desert was all that I could imagine. Finally, my daydreams and backyard imaginings were coming true. I was going to be a cowgirl!

The day dream and the reality could not have been farther apart.

Our family experience had a predictable beginning. The barn owner chose our horses based on experience level and temperament. My pestering was the reason for this equestrian experience that the rest of my family had to endure, and I was the first to mount up on my little gray pony. My favorite color! I knew we were meant to be, and I fell a little bit in love.

We stood waiting for the others in the shade of a tree, the flies dancing around us in the shadows. His tail and ears twitched impatiently as they buzzed quickly by, occasionally landing on me. I was in my glory. My little sister was mounted behind on a dark colored horse, perhaps black or bay. She was nervous. I can still picture it now. She didn't feel comfortable around horses, but she wanted to be like her big sister so she tried to hide her fear. My horse shifted weight as he dozed…and I panicked.

My sudden fear fed my sister's anxiety. She was following in her sister's footsteps and was taking my lead, trusting that she would be okay…until I lost my confidence. After all, I was the sister obsessed with horses. My being scared only signaled that there was something to truly be afraid of. The herd mentality was at work! I began to imagine that my little gray pony would panic and bolt with me on him, heading off into the vast desert with little old me on his back. I had never ridden independently and did not know my "whoa" from my "go." My fears fed my self-doubt and became crippling.

So here we were, two little girls sobbing on our ponies in the middle of the Arizona desert. I can only imagine what the other riders were thinking. I'm pretty sure my pony did not budge the entire time despite the wailing. Talk about patient and bombproof. We dismounted with help and refused to go on the trail.

This was a very disappointing beginning for a cowgirl.

My mother stayed with us in the yard while the others went into the desert. My father, a former Air Force Captain and war veteran, had no desire to ride horses. Ironically, he became the only member of our family to venture out that day. He came back a few hours later not wanting to speak about his experience. It was years later that I learned they encountered a rattlesnake on their adventure. He still is wary of horses to this day.

That day wasn't a total loss. I sat in that dusty Arizona paddock, grooming and loving on that pony, crying when I had to leave. I realized later that I let my fear of what could happen get in the way of something I really wanted to do, and I was disappointed in myself.

In retrospect, I would like to have done things differently. I regret not staying on that gray pony and riding off into the desert. I let my fear be greater than my passion. A desert ride is still on my equestrian bucket list.

The regret from our Arizona trip has eaten at me for years. My passion for horses didn't waiver; in fact, it grew. But there was always niggling doubt that I couldn't handle a horse.

This memory says a lot about me, none of which I'm very proud. I am nothing if not honest with myself and others. I am not embarrassed at the behavior of a young girl who was afraid of riding a strange horse in the Arizona desert. I had no riding experience at all. Zip. Zero. Zilch. But my horse didn't misbehave or give me any reason to be scared; my insecurities and vivid imagination did that all on its own.

It's a good reminder that one decision can have lasting consequences.

Like what you read? Order your copy of *Confessions of a Timid Rider* on Amazon.

APPENDIX

SOME OF MY FAVORITE PHOTOGRAPHS FROM MY TRAVELS.
WANT TO SEE MORE? MAKE SURE TO FOLLOW MY
ADVENTURES AT TIMIDRIDER.COM AND GOBIDESERT.COM.
EVEN BETTER, JOIN ME ON MY NEXT ADVENTURE IN
MONGOLIA.

Officials en route to base camp!

Checking my light settings.

Double rainbow at basecamp on Day 3! A wonderful omen for the day.

Queen of the hill on Day 4! Awaiting the riders at the checkpoint and looking for a good vantage point.

Beautiful Mongol horse on the traditional horse line. Custom dictates women must stay outside the horse line for safety reasons.

A traditional ger (often referred to as a yurt in Siberia), this is a portable nomadic home. My home, I shared with the other female officials for 10 days.

Commonly seen near roadsides, an ovoo or ceremonial stone shrine for travelers.

Local nomadic children showcased their wrestling skills for us at base camp.

Cantering across the steppe

Nomad games

Mongolian horsemanship is ancient and traditional in many ways. The Gobi Desert Cup works with the nomads to learn from and also introduce new methods for horse welfare.

A man and his giggling grandson. Generation after generation these families have lived a nomadic life with their animals, traveling to find food and water. This culture is slowly disappearing because of desertification. I'm proud to be part of an event working to hold on to these traditions and support a disappearing way of life. More, I'm grateful to be able to see if firsthand.

73403104R00116

Made in the
USA
Middletown, DE